LEADING
ORGANIZATIONS
THROUGH
TRANSITION

LEADING ORGANIZATIONS THROUGH TRANSITION

Communication and Cultural Change

Stanley A. Deetz
Sarah J. Tracy
Jennifer Lyn Simpson
In Cooperation with SETONWORLDWIDE

Sage Publications, Inc.
International Educational and Professional Publisher
Thousand Oaks ▪ London ▪ New Delhi

For information:

Sage Publications, Inc.
2455 Teller Road
Thousand Oaks, California 91320
E-mail: order@sagepub.com

Sage Publications Ltd.
6 Bonhill Street
London EC2A 4PU
United Kingdom

Sage Publications India Pvt. Ltd.
M-32 Market
Greater Kailash I
New Delhi 110 048 India

HD58.8
.D4325
2000
042643459

Printed in the United States of America

Library of Congress Cataloging-in-Publication Data

Deetz, Stanley
    Leading organizations through transition: Communication and cultural change / by Stanley A. Deetz, Sarah J. Tracy, and Jennifer Lyn Simpson.
        p. cm.
    Includes bibliographical references and index.
    ISBN 0-7619-2096-X (cloth: alk. paper)
    ISBN 0-7619-2097-8 (pbk.: alk. paper)
    1. Organizational change. 2. Corporate reorganizations.
    3. Communication in organizations. I. Tracy, Sarah J. II. Simpson, Jennifer Lyn. III. Title.
        HD58.8 .D4325 1999
        658.4'06—dc21   99-050466

This book is printed on acid-free paper.

00 01 02 03 04 05 06 7 6 5 4 3 2 1

Acquiring Editor:	Margaret H. Seawell
Editorial Assistant:	Brian Neumann
Production Editor:	Astrid Virding
Editorial Assistant:	Victoria Cheng
Typesetter/Designer:	Lynn Miyata
Indexer:	Cristina Haley
Cover Designer:	Candice Harman

Contents

▼

Introduction

▼

Success in business or by any organization today cannot be achieved by formula. Positive outcomes result from luck and unpredictable changes in tastes and markets as well as from creativity, hard work, and good management. Frequently, the best we can hope for is to increase the chances of being at the right place at the right time and being ready to meet the challenges once there. Positive business leaders face up to these real uncertainties and the lack of guarantees by promoting high levels of competence and adaptive learning environments in their companies.

The turbulent and unpredictable nature of the current business situation leads to increased concern with good communication skills. Making opportunities and making the most of opportunities requires developing high-performance workplaces filled with mutual responsibility, loyalty, and commitment to success. To succeed today requires less surveillance and supervision of employee behavior and more managing of hearts, minds, and souls—in short, managing culture.

This volume explores the process of building a business by exploring the relationship of cultural management to the overall business strategy and discussing the role of communication in cultural management. The various chapters discuss the role of leader communication in the formation and redevelopment of culture as an organization works through various changes, challenges, and opportunities.

▶ Leadership and Cultural Management

Leading by managing organizational culture has many benefits. More autonomy is experienced by individual employees and units. Creativity and feelings of ownership are increased. Important coordination and control can be achieved without direct managerial intervention. Not only are benefits clear, but as will become evident, in many workplaces today no other form of management is likely to succeed. High-performance workplaces have a character and a soul.

Managing culture requires special communication skills. A technically proficient manager has acquired trade-relevant knowledge and learned how to gather financial information, read trends, and instruct employees. But few managers have learned to lead, to inspire, or to understand the basis for employees' internal motivation and resistance. The communication and work habits that have lead them to be selected as managers are often quite different from those that enable them to succeed as leaders. Directing employee work activities is quite different from enabling and inspiring appropriate self-initiative. Presenting one's point of view persuasively is quite different from having employees spontaneously see the situation in a particular way on their own.

Cultural management, however, is not without potential downsides and controversies. IBM managers were praised in the early eighties for having produced a "strong culture" where employees were happy and committed and seemed to function as virtually one body. By the late eighties these same managers were criticized for a monolithic culture promoting groupthink and slow responses to a rapidly changing market.

Cultural management also raises a host of ethical questions. The very concept of managing minds, hearts, and souls evokes images of *1984*. The widely reported image of Microsoft employees happily giving up nights and weekends and family, community, and civic responsibilities to build Windows 95 may appear as a dream to some, but posed wider ethical and social responsibility issues. In an age of "spin doctors," cynicism abounds and the ability to distinguish insightful, productive reframing from politically opportunistic obscuring is an important skill.

The promotion of communication activities that help manage culture has to be balanced with concern for responsibility and the dilemmas of "empowering" others. The materials in this volume are developed to maintain balance and promote useful discussions of the various dilemmas inherent in cultural management. Communication is considered in both its strategic and its participatory forms. Strategic communication functions to direct, inspire, and coordinate and arises from a leader's vision or overall plan. Participatory communication, in contrast, is the process through which we create, invent, and innovate together. Here the direction and best choices are not yet known. They are best produced through talk. The balance between strategic and participatory communication helps produce an adaptive, ethical, and vibrant culture and helps distinguish valuable from unproductive employee resistance to change.

▶ **What This Book Does**

The primary purpose of this volume is to address the role of communication in organizational culture and cultural change efforts, especially during periods of transition, mergers, innovations, and globalization. The book is unabashedly normative and hopes to aid students and professionals in understanding and working with organizational cultural change.

Despite 20 years of cultural studies in the field of communication and increasing numbers of communication professionals and academics being called to work with organizational cultural change efforts, no book in the field has addressed communication and change efforts as a central theme. And although trade books and management texts have focused on cultural change, they have tended to be slim and superficial in the treatment of communication. Additionally, the best of these books have become quite dated and do not reflect contemporary situations and understandings.

The materials included in this book were initially developed as the electronic text for an online course in organizational culture and culture change as part of an executive master's program at Seton Hall University—SETONWORLDWIDE. The materials and course have been very successful with mid-level managers. The audience for the course, however, is greatly restricted. With the agreement and encouragement of SETONWORLDWIDE, we redeveloped the materials to work with a somewhat less sophisticated student and professional audience.

The material in the volume proceeds from relatively general issues related to communication, culture, and cultural change to specific practical contexts where these concepts are of value. Each chapter begins with common questions that guide the development of the chapter. We suggest considering them on your own before you begin your reading. You may also find it useful to pose your own related questions.

Case studies are used throughout to provide examples of organizational change efforts, highlight concerns raised in the text, and add the complexity of actual life choices. The cases are not meant simply to exemplify concepts but rather to pose issues for discussion with others. Additional cases are suggested at the end of several of the chapters.

▶ Overview of the Chapters

Chapter 1 introduces the relation between the leader's building a successful business and the management of culture. It begins with a consideration of how managing the workplace culture relates to the overall strategic development of a business. The chapter shows why the concern with culture has been a major feature of business thinking during the past 20 years and why this trend is likely to continue. Basic concepts are introduced that are used for the remainder of the volume.

Chapter 2 focuses on cultural assessment and change as a part of building a business and working in organizations. Included are discussions of what a positive culture accomplishes in the workplace, how one determines the appropriateness of the existing culture, and basic considerations in a change process.

Chapter 3 considers how business concepts, visions, or mission statements relate to building a business and the development and transformation of culture. Included are discussions of the characteristics of powerful visions, how one launches a vision campaign, how the vision can be connected to other workplace activities, and how one achieves buy-in from key employees. Finally, the chapter investigates how individuals invest their identity in the organization and explores ways to reward such investments.

Chapter 4 discusses the processes through which people develop their interpretations of events. Consideration is given to how a leader's values and perspective become embedded in the corporate culture. The discussion focuses on how language usage, stories, and ritual can shape, frame, or reframe employees' understandings of events.

Chapter 5 considers the various processes leading to the collaborative development of visions. The process of empowerment is developed. Strategic conversation and dialogue projects are shown to be useful in creating alternative futures and opening the business to the wider collective learning process. Widespread participation is shown to aid innovation as well as loyalty and commitment.

Chapter 6 explores a number of ethical issues in investigating and changing cultures. Cultural management raises a host of ethical questions. Are some cultures more ethical than others? How do cultural characteristics relate to the ethical behavior of members? What are the ethical issues related to cultural control and cultural assessment?

Chapter 7 looks at the probable impacts of the implementation of new technologies, especially information technologies, on cultures. The chapter considers the information management systems (IMS) subculture and its relation to wider organizational cultures, how technological innovation influences power dynamics, how particular cultures resist technological innovation, and how others overly idealize it. Special attention is given to how one works with cultural issues during technological implementation.

Chapter 8 looks at cultural changes and ways of managing culture during organizational transitions. Such transitions include the passing of the founder and other changes in top management, economic crises, and reengineering and reorganization activities as well as mergers and acquisition.

Chapter 9 introduces issues related to the globalization of business and the relations among multiple cultures. The chapter encourages the recognition of the possibility of multiple positive cultures, the development of multiple cultural forms of leadership, and the translation of visions into multiple cultural contexts. Special attention is given to intercultural communication and the relation of different and at times competing cultures in international organizations.

Chapter 10 provides a review and an extensive case focused on learning when to lead and when to manage, how to choose moments for intervention, and how to direct existing trends using the material developed in the book.

Acknowledgments

▼

As with any book, family and friends have provided critical help and support at many different stages. They each know how much we have appreciated it. A few we each credit specifically below. Furthermore, we want to acknowledge our students at CU-Boulder who listened patiently to ideas and provided several of the examples illustrated in this book. More specifically, Don McKenna of Seton Hall University initially solicited the materials for the SETONWORLDWIDE online course that became this book and provided valued comments on the materials. Patricia Sikora developed and allowed us to use the case study that forms the bulk of Chapter 10, as well as participated in useful discussions of change efforts. All the people at Sage Publications have made special efforts to bring this volume to a timely completion. Margaret Seawell in particular went well beyond the call of duty (and promised glue that lasts).

From Jen: My Mom and Dad, Mike and Carol Simpson, deserve special thanks for providing exemplary models of leadership during my early life. My brother Rob has encouraged, uplifted, poked fun, and provoked me to success more times than I can count. Thanks, again.

From Sarah: My parents, Malinda and Boyd, and my brother Van, as well as my religious faith, have sustained me throughout all my academic endeavors. For this I have the deepest gratitude. To Catherine, thank you for being a wonderful friend, and for telling me (sometimes not so gently) to "get back to work" whenever I procrastinate too long.

From Stan: A special thanks to Alexander, who lived around my hectic work schedule and finds fun and beauty in whatever the world tosses his way (and likes to see his name in print).

—Stanley A. Deetz, Sarah J. Tracy, and Jennifer Lyn Simpson
Boulder, Colorado

Managing Hearts, Minds, and Souls

Overview

Managing the hearts, minds, and souls of employees is a key element of building a successful business today. For the past 20 years this need has been loosely conceptualized as managing the "corporate culture."

Actually, the concerns this term highlights have been of interest to leaders for a long time. John Clemens (1986) traced the Western world's concern with corporate culture to a funeral oration by Pericles in 431 B.C. Pericles, now recognized as the father of Athens's Golden Age, was attempting to inspire unity in his people in their battle with Sparta. The speech effectively displayed the two central elements of establishing a strong corporate culture: determining what makes the organization different and eloquently communicating those differences to the organizational members.

At least since that time, scholars and managers have tried to get a handle on the elusive subjective side of work life. Whether the concern has been with "spirit," "climate," "meaning of work," or "quality of work life," the core issues have been the same. Human beings are more than rational creatures. They are not animated machines. How employees personally feel, think, and see the company and their work have a significant impact on the character and quality of their work, their relation to management, and their response to innovation and change. Culture is a concept many have found useful and necessary to understanding, managing, and strategically changing organizations.

This chapter provides an introduction to the role of communication in developing and transforming corporate culture. First, the culture concept is developed in relation to the overall plan of building a business. Second is a discussion of the social, economic, and historical changes that have accentuated the concern with corporate culture in recent years. Third, the roots of the organizational culture approach in business are discussed. Finally, the concept of culture is developed in such a way as to aid our attention to the values and decisional premises that underlie organizational behavior and highlight different assumptions people make about the nature of others and work.

Key Objectives of the Chapter

▼ To develop the capacity to integrate cultural concerns in the overall business plan

▼ To recognize the conditions leading to the need to manage culture

▼ To recognize the external and internal factors contributing to specific cultural characteristics in an organization

▼ To identify different culture *sites* or *levels*

▼ To begin to examine how underlying values and decisional premises influence behavior and decisions in actual workplaces

▼ To recognize differences in the character of different cultures and the relation to work activities

▼ To recognize the fundamentally different assumptions people make about their work world and the consequences for leadership.

Questions to Consider

▼ When you build a strategic plan, how do you take into account human factors?

▼ How can various activities of an organization be difficult to coordinate?

▼ Do you feel that members of organizations you are involved in "walk their talk"? If so, where is this most evident? If not, what have been the consequences?

▼ Do you think that the wider national culture greatly influences the productivity of employees and companies?

▼ Do you think people naturally enjoy quality work? Do authority structures, reward systems, task quality, or intangibles of work life have the greatest influence on employee commitment and productivity?

▶ ## Managing Culture as a Part of the Overall Strategic Plan

A successful business strategy results from a number of key considerations. First, market conditions largely determine the possible financial success of the selling of any good or service. Identification of and customizing the product to a particular market niche is central to building any business. Second, control of critical performance variables is central to keeping production costs down and meeting the challenge of potential competitors. Third, adequate monitoring of the environment and making adaptive changes is essential to continued success under changing resource and market conditions. Finally, a workforce must be recruited and developed in ways that support the aforementioned needs.

The Relation Between Strategy and Culture

The corporate culture is not just one of many considerations in building a business. Rather the culture impacts on each of the strategic dimensions listed above. The way organizational members think and feel influences the relation to the market, workplace performance, adaptability, and workforce development and commitment. A positive business strategy and positive corporate culture go hand in hand. An effective strategy must grow out of the culture and the culture must be strategically shaped.

A positive workplace culture actualizes the latent potential in all members and reduces the need for managerial intervention and direction. All employees have the potential to contribute, do right, achieve, and create. Accomplishing each of these potentials can be thwarted by various organizational blocks. The desire to contribute is blocked by uncertainty about purpose. The desire to do right is limited by work pressures and the temptation to serve one's self. The desire to achieve can be sidetracked by lack of focus or of resources. And the desire to create cannot be fulfilled if opportunities are lacking or there is a fear of risk.

Actualizing these potentials requires both a business strategy and appropriate cultural conditions. The ability of an employee to contribute is enhanced by the effective communication of core values and mission. The ability to do right is aided by specifying and enforcing of the rules of the game. The ability to achieve is supported by carefully built and supported targets. And the ability to create is stimulated by open organizational dialogue to encourage learning.

If support for these potentials is built into the corporate culture, the need for direct intervention by upper managers is lessened and commitment, autonomy, and motivation are increased. The old view of business called for direct managerial supervision. Employees were seen as needing to be motivated, pushed, or coerced into meeting business objectives. Compliance was an endless issue. A corporate culture was developed and reinforced that required more of the same. The new cultural view says that employees are not inherently lazy and resistant, nor are they naturally motivated and open to change. The nature of the employee is a cultural product. A positive corporate culture creates employee potentials and the context in which they can be realized.

> Culture enhances social integration; social integration eliminates the need for bureaucracy, and increases levels of investment which, in turn, enhance performance and productivity. Thus, by manipulating culture, substantial increments in profitability should accrue.
> —*Gideon Kunda and Stephen Barley (1988, p. 21)*

Why Lead by Managing Culture?

Successful business leaders have gradually moved from traditional forms of management, primarily based in hierarchical decision making and managerial supervision and control, to managing by managing culture. Many reasons exist for this change. They have to do with structural, social, and market changes. As long as these new conditions persist, the competitive advantage will continue to go to businesses that focus on the corporate culture.

The most obvious, and best understood, reason for the change to managing corporate culture was the perception that some cultures lead to greater productivity than others. In the late 1970s, managers in the United States saw increasing economic difficulties in their companies largely arising from Japanese competition. Even superficial analyses revealed that cultural features were a major reason why Japanese workers were more productive and their products of higher quality. At that time, the stronger, clanlike corporate cultures of Japan provided production innovations and worker dedication unmatched by American companies. American managers rushed to learn the Japanese way and companies in the United States with strong cultures were suddenly highlighted. The success of Japanese companies, viewed partly as a result of their cultural distinctiveness, encouraged Western managers to analyze how their corporations could make better use of team spirit, corporate pride, and worker morale.

More subtle changes were taking place, however, that may account for the Japanese success at that time and the fact that cultural management has persisted longer than the Japanese success story. Important social changes and changes in the nature of products and work processes provided management with a crisis of control. The rise of professionalized workplaces, geographically dispersed facilities, decentralization, and turbulent markets contributed to the difficulty of coordination and control. As is explored in Chapter 2, each of these conditions makes corporate culture of more interest.

In the face of these changes, the use of more indirect and unobtrusive control through cultural management offers possibilities and advantages not shared by traditional activities. In fact, many workplaces could not function at all without a strong shared culture. Most of these new social realities are not likely to go away. Cultural management will continue to be a key feature of successful business for some time. Cultural management presents a different form of leadership, a form understood in Eastern cultures for some time:

The Way of Lao Tzu, Number 17

The best (rulers) are those whose existence is (merely)
known by the people.
The next best are those who are loved and praised.
The next are those who are feared.
The next are those who are despised.
It is only when one does not have enough faith in others
that others have no faith in him.
(The great rulers) value their words highly.
They accomplish their task; they complete their work.
Nevertheless their people say that they simply follow nature.
—*4th/6th century* B.C. *(1963, p. 130)*

If the leader used few but carefully chosen words, the way will seem natural and people will feel that the methods and accomplishments are their own.

Exercise 1.1

- How can organizations contribute to the member's potential to contribute, to do right, to achieve, and to create?

- When you consider yourself as a member of an organization (including an academic or university community), to what extent do you believe that your department's administration has considered your beliefs and values? In what ways have these been taken into account? In which ways have they been ignored or glossed over?

▶ ## Historical Roots of the Cultural Approach

> This ability to perceive the limitations of one's own culture and to de-velop the culture adaptively is the essence and ultimate challenge of leadership. The most important message for leaders at this point is "Try to understand culture, give it its due, and ask yourself how well you can begin to understand the culture in which you are embedded."
>
> —*Edwin Schein (1992, p. 2)*

Until a shift in focus during the early 1980s, most organizational scholars and leaders strove to provide a scientific, objective, and causal under-standing of organizations. Organizational studies measured outcomes—such as productivity, effectiveness, and employee satisfaction—so that they could be predicted and controlled in the future. In this tradition, organizational metaphors were patterned after the scientific approach and businesses were compared to machines or systems. These meta-phors led researchers and practitioners to conceive of communication as just another variable that could be understood through the lenses of in-put and output rather than an important phenomenon in and of itself.

A Scholarly Approach to Culture

This traditional approach came under fire in the late 1970s as organi-zational scholars began to develop the organizational cultural approach. Whereas the traditional approach compares organizations to machines, those interested in culture use analogies that compare organizations to clans or tribes. The underlying motive of the organizational cultural approach is to understand and learn how organizational life is accomplished through communication. Inherent in this view is that meanings do not reside in messages, channels, or texts on screens; rather they unfold through social interaction and sense-making activities of people.

In the academy, the ideas of organizational culture draw quite heavily from the field of anthropology, with one of the leading proponents of this interpretive approach being the anthropologist Clifford Geertz. Cultural theorists attempt to provide vivid descriptive accounts of organizational life and concern themselves with articulating the recurrent themes that specify the links among values, beliefs, and action in an organization. According to anthropologist K. L. Gregory (1983), who studied knowledge-intensive companies in Silicon Valley, the corporate world is just as wondrous, strange, and exotic and full of specialized meanings and significance as a remote village on the other side of the Himalayas. Thinking about the organization as a clan or tribe with an exotic culture can lead to important new insights.

The Business World Catches the Culture Craze

Three groundbreaking books had an unprecedented impact on American corporate leaders. Since their publication in the early 1980s, business books have skyrocketed in popularity. These three best-sellers appeared during a time of international competition and domestic economic turbulence. The books helped corporate leaders to focus on organizational values, visions, and leadership, concepts that are integral to the culture management approach.

William Ouchi's Theory Z. The first book to popularize the concept of organizational culture was William Ouchi's *Theory Z* (1981). Ouchi's book explained how corporate success correlated with the organization's ability to adjust to its surrounding national culture(s) and its particular standards for excellence. The primary conclusion of his analysis was that the best type of an organization (a "Theory Z" type) would integrate the values of individual achievement and advancement common to U.S. organizations with the sense of community so common in the Japanese workplace.

Terrence Deal and Allan Kennedy's Corporate Cultures. Another best-seller that analyzed organization culture was Terrence Deal and Allan Kennedy's *Corporate Cultures: The Rites and Rituals of Corporate Life* (1982). Whereas Ouchi (1981) focused on values and norms ascribed to particular national cultures, Deal and Kennedy detailed the varying components that make up a "strong" culture. They identified five: (a) the business's external environment, (b) organizational values, (c) organizational heroes, (d) rites and rituals, and (e) the cultural network.

Tom Peters and Robert Waterman's In Search of Excellence. The third book that brought culture to the forefront of corporate thought was Tom Peters and Robert Waterman's *In Search of Excellence* (1982). The authors analyzed 62 companies that had been described as "excellent" by journalists, scholarly experts, and employees. They found eight common themes that illustrated these businesses' cultures: (a) a bias for action; (b) close to the customer; (c) autonomy and entrepreneurship; (d) productivity through people; (e) hands-on, value-driven; (f) stick to the knitting; (g) simple form, lean staff; and (h) simultaneously loose-tight properties.

From the brief descriptions of these books, a preliminary idea of what culture is emerges. Nevertheless, its definition is in no way explicit or clear-cut, and researchers continue to argue about how culture should best be understood.

▶ Basic Elements of Corporate Culture

Culture has been described as everything from common systems of values, beliefs, and norms to collections of shared social knowledge. The organizational culture construct is derived from that used in anthropology, yet even here scholars have disagreed on its definition. The anthropologist Clifford Geertz (1973) defines culture as "the fabric of meaning in terms of which human beings interpret their experience and guide their action; social structure is the form that action takes, the actually existing network of social relations" (p. 145). Geertz compares culture to a spiderweb that people spin through their everyday communication with each other.

Some have argued that it is difficult for the organizational theorist to borrow the cultural construct in its entirety. Be that as it may, the construct continues to be widely used in the study of organizations. Edwin Schein (1992, p. 9) outlines some of the most widely used conceptions of culture. They include observed behavioral regularities when people interact (e.g., language, traditions, rituals); group norms, standards, and values; espoused or articulated values; formal philosophy; rules of the "game"; learning the organizational "ropes"; climate, or the feeling portrayed through organization's physical layout and the way people relate with each other; embedded skills or the special abilities of the organization (not necessarily articulated in writing); habits of thinking, mental models, and other linguistic paradigms; shared meanings; and "root metaphors," or integrating symbols. Linda Smircich and Marta Calás (1987) suggest that we should not think of culture as some kind of thing, container, or possession. They argue that culture is not what an organization *has*; rather, it represents what an organization *is*.

Culture: Two Worldviews

One major division in the culture approach is whether primacy should be on internal psychological factors (such as underlying beliefs, assumptions, and unconscious mental frameworks) or whether we should focus more on external factors (such as behavior, language, physical artifacts, and company rhetoric). With this question of primacy, another question emerges. Do internal values create external behaviors and communication patterns, or do external actions create people's internal assumptions and beliefs?

In the first worldview, cultural change is conceived of as emanating from internal, deep value change. As Ouchi (1981) says, "A culture changes slowly because its values reach deeply and integrate into a consistent network of beliefs that tend to maintain the status quo" (quoted in Schein, 1992, p. 75). A basic assumption of this view is that an organization can best change its habits and actions by first changing its employees' internal values and belief structures.

In the second worldview, the focus is on external behaviors, actions, and communication patterns as shaping and forming internal values and beliefs. According to this view, the best way to go about changing an organization's culture is to first change its everyday habits, communication patterns, and espoused goals. For instance, the psychologist Daryl J. Bem (1972) developed a "self perception" theory that argues that people first observe their behaviors and communication and then conclude that they hold values that uphold their earlier actions (Bem, 1972). In this

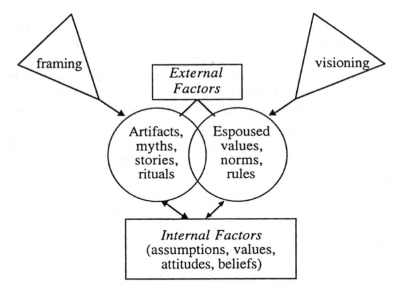

Figure 1.1. The Culture Process

NOTE: Managers can control everyday communication and espoused values through framing and visioning. This, in turn, can affect underlying assumptions. The more the two spheres overlap, the more closely behavior is congruent with the articulated goals of the organization.

view, an organization can be regarded as a system of symbols that socially construct peoples' values. These symbols, or discursive instruments, create order and clarity out of chaos. Examples range from verbal symbols such as organizational myths, jokes, stories, slogans, and corporate logos to material elements such as the physical layout of work and office space, exterior design, and the designation of parking spaces for employees.

An Integrated Approach

A useful alternative view is more extensive, and admittedly fuzzier, than the two world views described above. In this alternative view, culture is inherently implicated in both what we *do* and how we *think* about what we do. Culture is made up of and mutually constituted by both the internal and the external; values affect behaviors, and behaviors affect values. Together, the two create organizational culture. Thus, culture should not be thought of as a product that an organization has; rather culture is the ongoing process of what an organization is (see Figure 1.1.).

Although internal and external elements are equally important in making up a culture, organizational leaders have more direct control in shaping communication patterns and overt behaviors than they do in changing deep-rooted value systems. Therefore, much of this book's focus will be on how leaders can create and change a culture through the way they communicate. Chapter 3 examines how leaders can affect the espoused values, norms, and rules of their organization through visioning and how this can shape employees' identification with the organization. Chapter 4 focuses on how managers can best frame organizational stories, myths, and everyday communication so that they are in line with the values that are best for the organization.

In summary, culture can be considered to be a set of loosely structured symbols that are maintained and co-created by a recreative pattern of internal factors (such as attitudes, beliefs, assumptions, and ideologies) and external factors (such as language, behaviors, espoused values, and physical artifacts). These symbols, and an absence of other symbols, help make sense of organizational members' shared (and unshared) values, beliefs, and assumptions.

Exercise 1.2

Describe an experience where you have been involved with an organization where people talked about or espoused one set of values, but behaved in a way that exemplified other values.

* What kinds of beliefs and values dominated this organization's formal literature (organizational mission, rules, and regulations)?

* What kinds of beliefs, values, and topics dominated informal communication and everyday organizational member behavior?

* Were the organization's espoused values congruent with the employees' or members' everyday behaviors?

* What does this tell you about this organization?

Think of three influential people in an organization with which you are familiar.

* In what ways do they symbolize the character of the organization?

* Are their actions more in line with the organization's explicit mission or with informal organizational myths?

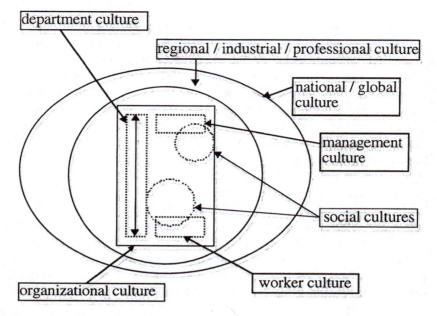

Figure 1.2. Culture Levels

▶ Cultural Sites and Levels

Culture is not something that is easy to control. One of the central difficulties of managing culture is understanding the multiple organizational
subcultures and countercultures. By focusing on one distinct overriding
culture, the manager can lose sight of the great likelihood that there are
overlapping (and sometimes conflicting) cultures that coexist at different
levels and sectors in any organization. Thus, multiple values simultaneously compete in their goal of shaping the organization (see Figure 1.2).
The first step in managing these cultures is being able to identify and
understand them.

National Culture

At the macro level, organizational leaders must be aware of cultural
differences across nations. Customs that seem normal and natural in one
nation may be unnatural and even offensive in another. Chapters 8 and
9 specifically speak to how organizational leaders should recognize the

possibility of multiple cultures and how they can translate their organizational vision into multiple cultural contexts.

Regional, Industrial, and Professional Cultures

At the next level are the regional, industrial, and professional cultures. Some organizations have a particular sense of identity and a special way of thinking that is specific to their geographical area. This is true in the case of businesses located in Silicon Valley, California. In this region, the values of innovation and diligence thrive in a way unparalleled in the rest of the country, and this has caused the area to boom with knowledge-intensive, cutting-edge companies. Certain industries (e.g., auto industry) and professions (e.g., doctors, lawyers, public relations practitioners) also have distinct cultures that may be similar to or different from a particular organizational culture. For instance, the agriculture industry has different values from the auto industry. Likewise, most doctors tend to keep the Hippocratic oath as a first priority, whereas lawyers are socialized to value the client/lawyer privilege.

Corporate Culture

The next level of organizational culture, that of the corporation or business itself, is the one most questioned and analyzed. Using a culture approach, organizations are viewed metaphorically as "clans," "tribes," or "living organisms." Although a certain organization may have several overall values (such as "total quality") that run throughout the company, most of the time subcultures exist throughout the organization.

Subcultures: Hierarchical Levels, Departments, Social Groups

Subcultures can be found hierarchically and departmentally. The values that characterize the thinking of upper management may be very different from those that characterize the assembly line workers. For instance, automobile company management may have cost cutting at the top of its list of values, whereas assembly line workers may have the value of "a fair day's wage for a fair day's work" as their first priority. Likewise, values vary in each department. Engineers tend to have different priorities and values from accountants, salespeople, and machine operators, for example. In addition, "social" subcultures cross over hierarchical and departmental lines. This is true, for instance, when a certain configuration of employees all play on the organization's softball team or attend the same church.

Because every organization is filled with subcultures, it is naive and erroneous for top management to assume that its culture (which includes its values and priorities) automatically permeates or even "trickles down" to other parts of the organization. This is why communication, whether through visioning (Chapter 3), framing (Chapter 4), or dialogue (Chapter 5), is vital to shaping and modifying a strong corporate culture. It is through communication that managers can shape and modify organizational culture.

Exercise 1.3

- The culture of an organization is encoded in the internal values and external behaviors that give form to everyday experience. Think about an organization with which you are familiar. How would you describe its culture?

- Identify subcultures in this organization. How are they differentiated? Are they in conflict or harmony? What impact do these subcultures have on shaping the organization? What functions do these groupings serve for their members? Is their overall effect on the organization positive or negative?

- How is culture communicated through this organization formally and informally?

▶ **Culture in the Contemporary Workplace**

Culture performs a number of very important functions in most contemporary workplaces. Understanding the way culture influences the workplace helps show the importance of it and provides some insight into when development and change are necessary. Following Vijay Sathe's (1985) work, coordination, decision making, control, motivation and commitment, and justification will be considered.

Coordination

Decentralized decision making, increased use of cross-functional teams, and professionals working at remote sites make surveillance of the work effort and coordination of decisions very difficult. Shared values can provide coordination and invisible management. With a strong culture, individuals and groups with little direct contact can make passively-coordinated decisions because their decisions are made using the same premises and values. Upper management does not have to anticipate all contingencies if similar underlying values and assumptions guide the decisions of diverse groups. Furthermore, strong cultures tend to generate identification with the organization and greater trust of other groups and members. This in turn increases the amount and clarity of communication and aids coordination.

Decision Making

Basic assumptions and values enter into decision making in a variety of ways. Business decisions are nearly always made under conditions of great uncertainty. Information is often incomplete and changes in environments are not always knowable. Values and assumptions fill in the gap between what one knows and the need for a decision now. Values are deeply involved in decision making even where uncertainty is less. Basic questions of what should be produced, what risks are to be assumed, and how a problem should be handled are not answered by knowing more but are based on preferences and values. In most cases organizations develop rather routine decisional premises that are deeply embedded in culture-based activities that implement these values and preferences in an invisible way. Culture matters.

Control

Workplaces today suffer from both too much control, which stifles creativity, innovation, and shared responsibility, and too little control, which makes coordination and direction difficult. Culture can be responsible for both.

Some workplaces have experienced a crisis of control in part owing to the decline in the strength of external cultures. For most of the 20th century, work relations have assumed a stable and consensual set of values and moral standards given by the wider society. Traditionally in the Western world, the so-called Protestant work ethic provided an important extra-organizational motivational form. Basic standards of hard work, honesty, belief in quality and standards, and accurate reporting provided a voluntary conformity to social practices. The general expectation and support of these has declined in contemporary society. Certainly work processes and corporate effects on other institutions have been partially responsible for this decline in workers' as well as managers' and owners' commitment to shared values. Corporate culture can provide values and direction in the face of the changing and often weakening external culture.

Traditional forms of control are often structurally limited in modern workplaces. Surveillance is often difficult, responsibility is hard to fix, and the costs of member disruptions and even sabotage are great in many industries. Inappropriate activities, resistance, and rule violation can create problems, since corporations have generally relied on voluntary compliance with rules and internal regulations. With sophisticated equipment, common data banks, and highly coordinated processes, these acts are considerably more costly and harder to blame on someone. Although increased monitoring is likely in many corporations, surveillance is costly in itself and often fosters an environment where increased disruption is likely. Control from a strong culture and resultant acts of self-surveillance are obviously a solution preferred by most management groups.

Culture provides powerful and often invisible control. For this reason it is valued in workplaces today. But as will be discussed, it can also reduce creativity, innovation, and adaptability precisely because of power and invisibility. In addition, managers need to distinguish between cultural control and brainwashing. Although leaders can do much to inculcate their values in employees, they must also allow for feedback and dialogue, issues that are dealt with more specifically in the later chapter on ethics.

Motivation and Commitment

Explicit systems of rewards and sanctions are difficult to administer in the modern organization, especially with team processes and highly integrated activities. The supervisor frequently lacks the "trade-relevant knowledge" necessary to assess the employee's effort. Sanctions in most day-to-day operations are difficult to assign, often have negative side effects, and usually end up appearing capricious. Rewards in even the more obvious cases of sales commissions are often complicated by the effects of support staffs, engineers, and others traditionally outside of the sales process. Monitoring the amount and quality of work in the service industries becomes increasingly difficult. And supervisors often lack the authority to reward meaningfully except in unusual cases. A positive corporate culture reduces the need for the type of motivation and direction thought to be gained from supervision and reward and punishment systems.

A positive culture increases self-management and increases the commitment and motivations arising from the individuals and teams themselves. When a person feels emotional attachment to and identifies with the business, he or she feels greater commitment and is more motivated. A committed employee is more likely to base choices on the perceived good of the company and find ways to accomplish personal objectives within the parameters of the overall business objectives.

Justification

Complexity, distant financial imperatives (and manipulations), white-collar layoffs, and changing attitudes to authority challenge the felt legitimacy of the company and upper management. After a couple of decades of leveraged buyouts, reorganizations, reengineering, mergers, and downsizing/rightsizing/upsizing, many employees are quite cynical. The sense of trust that came with the assumed contract of lifetime employment and the confidence that upper managers and owners had the best interests of the company rather than themselves in mind has largely disappeared. Traditional figures of authority have been questioned and even ridiculed. Authority has lost its mystique and is more clearly seen as arbitrary.

It is difficult for the large corporation to mimic the characteristic of the family firm and thus to achieve the loyalty and personal identification frequently attributed to it. The lack of personal contact places greater demands on reason giving and explicit justifications, but these become increasingly abstract and hidden from view. Decentralization, widespread decisional participation, and explicit cultural management are necessary to reclaim legitimacy in most businesses.

▶ Character and Strength of Culture

Corporate cultures differ in both their character and their strength. Both have significant influence on workplace performance and on change efforts. *Character of culture* refers to the specific values, beliefs, and activities that compose a culture. *Strength of culture* refers to the amount of overlapping support and sites providing repetition of dominant cultural elements as well as the intensity of member identifications with the culture. The character of the culture provides the direction of cultural impact and the strength of the culture provides its force.

Character of Culture

Many of the "sites" of culture influence the particular culture of an organization. The founders of the organization carry in cultural elements as they initially structure, hire, and manage the company. They bring in a pattern of values, assumptions, and practices they have drawn from their own experiences and their national, regional, ethnic, religious, occupational, and professional communities. Employees may be selected who fit well in the founder's life world, but inevitably they bring varying cultural orientations from their own experiences and communities. Depending on the relative strength of the founders and the various external communities, a culture emerges as an amalgamation of different proportions or cultural forces. Part of the business may differ in what emerges based on the relative identification with the founder and the strength of occupations and professional groups.

Business experience also influences the culture. Periods of nationalism or specific events in the history of the company can change the relative strength of different influential elements. Corporate cultures, although relatively stable, are influenced by organizational learning, training programs, and environmental events. Bell Laboratories, for example, has maintained many features but still is a very different place today from a couple of decades ago. In the past 20 years Bell Labs has changed from a university-like research center in a regulated monopoly, to a market-driven R&D operation in AT&T after divestiture, to an innovative technology company as Lucent Technologies. Much efforts and resources have been put into these changes and many employees have left who would not or could not adapt to the new culture. But change happens.

Many researchers have developed typologies to describe differences in cultural character. Each of these draw attention to the particular cultural differences that make a difference. Focusing on character differences helps match particular cultural characteristics to specific business needs, aids the understanding of cultural clashes, and directs activities in change efforts.

Geert Hofstede and his associates (Hofstede, Neuijen, Ohayv, & Sanders, 1990) have conducted extensive studies of cultures in different countries. They suggest that it is meaningful to account for differences based on differences in conventions, customs, habits, and mores. They identified the following six dimensions of difference:

1. Process-oriented versus results-oriented

2. Employee-oriented versus job-oriented

3. Parochial versus professional (do employees identify primarily with their own company or their own professions)

4. Open versus closed systems of communication

5. Loose versus tight (bureaucratic) control

6. Normative versus pragmatic (presses own view of the world versus responsive to customers) (p. 303)

Sue Cartwright and Cary Cooper (1992), considering this and other studies, describe four prototypical cultures. These will be used later in looking at the likely consequences of mergers and other changes that bring different cultures into contact.

Power Cultures. Power cultures are usually found in organizations where power is centralized in a few individuals, often founders or others central to developing the organization. Usually, these have easily identified leaders who like to make quick dramatic changes, often based in intuition. Such cultures thrive on personal loyalty to leaders, with reward and punishment structures often reflecting favoritism and perceived loyalties. Tradition is usually visibly present. Employees may feel personal commitment and loyalty but also disempowered, and they often experience low morale and lack ownership of decisions.

Role Cultures. Role cultures are usually fairly bureaucratic and emphasize logic, rationality, and the achievement of efficiency. Policy manuals are important and often fairly thick. One's role becomes one's principal source of identity. Individuals tend to become very status conscious with much open competition between organizational units. Employees frequently feel relatively secure in such cultures but lack innovation and risk taking. Such cultures are especially resistant to change and often do not adapt well to new environmental conditions.

Task or Achievement Cultures. Task or achievement cultures are characterized by flexibility and high levels of employee autonomy. They tend to lack strong formal structures. Team decision making is prized. The task becomes the primary organizing feature. Control and coordination tend to be ad hoc, aiding innovation but also creating difficulties of a common response, especially in times of crises.

Person/Support Cultures. Person/support cultures tend to be egalitarian. The personal growth and development of the individual is treated as equally important as business objectives. These cultures tend to be long term in focus, expecting to realize the human investment over a long period of time. Decision making tends to be collective and based on multiple needs of people and business.

Exercise 1.4

Complete the Sample Culture Assessment Test at the end of the chapter (Appendix 1.1).

Strength of Culture

The stronger the culture, the more impact it can have on employee commitment and performance and on corporate decisions. This can be both good and bad. A strong culture appropriate to the business mission and in tune with current environmental conditions can greatly enhance the company's performance and employee well-being. But in other circumstances, a strong culture can hamper performance and be quite resistant to change.

The strength of a culture is determined by several factors. First is the degree of redundancy. Redundancy is the number of different systems impacting on organizational members that share cultural characteristics. If company values are consistent with national and community values and with different levels in the organization and across the industry, the strength of the culture is increased. If the various systems are contradictory, the strength is reduced.

Second, the degree of integration increases strength. Cultural strength is increased when company values are carefully integrated with deeply held values of employees. Furthermore, cultural strength is increased when pay systems, employee relations, and espoused values are consistent.

Both redundancy and integration make company values and practices more thoroughly internalized by all organizational members and more likely owned by members. Weak cultures are more likely to be seen as arbitrary or contrived and may evoke compliance but less commitment.

Exercise 1.5

* Discuss the strength of the culture in an organization with which you are familiar.

* Would a stronger or weaker culture better meet organizational goals? Member goals?

▶ Culture and Fundamental Assumptions

Culture is not like taste, fashion, or opinion. Culture involves the most basic assumptions people make about the nature of their world and the people in it. It includes their most basic ideas of what is proper and moral. To mess with these things is not just to change a person's attitude at work, it impacts on the sensefulness of the world—what is fair, how things should work. One of the reasons culture management is so powerful is because individual attitudes and ideologies often operate beyond conscious awareness. Because most people understand their assumptions to be normal, natural, and right, they do little to question their basic beliefs—something that can have both positive and negative implications. Schein (1992) details the types of deeply held assumptions people hold about reality, time, space, human nature, and human relationships.

Assumptions About Reality

People differ in their views on reality and what is morally right. Although some people behave in ways that respect the spiritual or religious world as "real," others do not. People also differ in what they believe a certain concept or idea "counts" as (e.g., what is interpreted as war, unethical behavior, or success?). Although some people require significant amounts of data to prove an argument, others are happy to believe in a concept based on one person's testimony. Some assume that decisions should be based on universal rules, whereas others espouse a more experiential ethic.

Assumptions About Time

Like assumptions about reality, assumptions about time often only surface when people's assumptions clash. For instance, people differ on what they consider to be "on time," "time wasted," "enough time to plan ahead," "too much work in too little time," or a proper "learning curve time." Cultures also differ on whether they focus on past mistakes, present "to do" lists, or future goals. Assumptions can differ in regard to linearity of time. Whereas some people insist on doing "one thing at a time," others juggle multiple projects simultaneously. Frustration can erupt when these two types of people come into contact with each other (e.g., consider the last time you were waiting "forever" for a doctor because you did not realize she or he was seeing three patients at a time).

Assumptions About Space

Use of space tells us a lot about people's relationships and their status level. People make assumptions about intimacy based on how close someone stands to another person. Like all assumptions, though, no single definition of proper personal space holds true across cultures, and confusion or irritation can occur when people with different assumptions meet. What it means to "intrude" can also change across cultures. Whereas in the United States it is generally fine to stand in a person's line of view, in other cultures this would be considered to be as forceful as a verbal interruption.

Last, space indicates status. Generally, large corner offices with big windows and closed doors indicate high status. When this rule is "broken" it is very symbolic. Such is the case at a company Schein (1992) calls "Action," where secretaries are given the prime window offices. This decision about office space strongly symbolizes the way the company values and appreciates the important, but often monotonous, work its secretaries must perform.

Assumptions About Human Nature

Assumptions about human nature can have a tremendous effect on the ways people work and lead in organizations. Douglas McGregor (1960) labeled two distinct orientations as "Theory X" and "Theory Y." People who lead by Theory X believe workers do not really enjoy work, are only motivated by financial rewards, have little initiative, and thus must be tightly supervised. Leaders who operate under a Theory Y point of view, on the other hand, believe that workers generally enjoy work, are motivated by a variety of needs, desire autonomy and creativity, and thus do not require close supervision.

People also differ in their beliefs about human agency. Some people believe they have control over their environment and organizational world, whereas others believe humans to be victims or products of societal and organizational structures. The particular framework a person operates under can greatly effect day-to-day operations of an organization, such as the types of work incentives given and the amount of participatory decision making encouraged.

Assumptions About Human Relationships

People differ in their assumptions about how people should behave in groups. In Western societies, there is an emphasis on individual achievement, originality, and competition. Most Asian cultures, on the other hand, focus on group unity, family pride, and societal cooperation. When these cultures come together, there can be problems. These assumptions affect the structure of organizational hierarchies, division of duties, and compensation.

Together, the above assumptions about reality, time, space, human nature, and human relationships make up rules of interaction—determining what counts as "right" and "appropriate." One of the reasons such assumptions are so powerful is because they are deeply held and often beyond conscious recognition. Nevertheless, these basic beliefs frame the ways that people go about their lives. They come to the surface often only when they clash with the assumptions of others. This is one reason why it is so important that a culture know itself before it decides to change or merge with another culture.

Cultural assumptions are strongly held by most people. Before the change process is considered in the next chapter, you may wish to consider moments when your own view of how things work or what is right and fair were challenged. Consider the death of a young parent or child, your feelings about the justice system after the OJ verdict or a divorce settlement, the first time you were offered dog or cat to eat, the promotion given for political reasons when you were more qualified, times when children shoot children at school. If you can think of such situations, it is easier to understand the horror and disbelief when culture change is attempted and the accompanying sense that the gods must be crazy.

Exercise 1.6

- Describe your personal beliefs about people and the way they are motivated to work.

- Imagine that you were caught in a Jim Carrey liar sequence with a new employee where you always told the truth. What would you say?

- Describe the real rules of life as you see them in most companies.

 ## Review Questions

▼ What role does culture play in the development of a business strategy?

▼ Why did the culture approach emerge?

▼ What are the advantages of a strong culture?

▼ How could a strong culture be limiting?

▼ What culture sites or levels make up a culture?

▼ What actions can managers take in communicating culture?

▼ What are some of the basic assumptions that make up people's value structures?

Discussion Questions

▼ What do you consider to be the virtues and problems of managing by "hearts, minds, and souls"?

▼ Do you think that workplace coordination and control are more difficult today? If so, where and when? What evidence do you have?

▼ Why do deeply held assumptions about reality, time, space, human nature, and human relationships usually only come to the surface when they clash with another's assumptions? What are some instances when you have become aware of your own deeply held assumptions?

References and Recommended Readings

Barley, S., Meyer, G., & Gash, D. (1988). Cultures of culture: Academics, practitioners and the pragmatics of normative control. *Administrative Science Quarterly, 33,* 24-60.

Bem, D. (1972). *Beliefs, attitudes and human affairs.* Belmont, CA: Wadsworth.

Cartwright, S., & Cooper, C. (1992). *Mergers and acquisitions: The human factor.* Oxford, UK: Butterworth, Heinemann.

Clemens, J. (1986, October 13). A lesson from 431 B.C. *Fortune,* pp. 161, 164.

Deal, T., & Kennedy, A. (1982). *Corporate cultures: The rites and rituals of corporate life.* Reading, MA: Addison-Wesley.

Geertz, C. (1973). *The interpretation of cultures.* New York: Basic Books.

Gregory, K. L. (1983). Native-view paradigms: Multiple cultures and culture conflicts in organizations. *Administrative Sciences Quarterly, 28,* 359-376.

Hofstede, G., Neuijen, B., Ohayv, D., & Sanders, G. (1990). Measuring organizational cultures. *Administrative Science Quarterly, 35,* 286-316.

Kunda, G. (1992). *Engineering culture.* Philadelphia: Temple University Press.

Kunda, G., & Barley, S. (1988, August). *Designing devotion: Corporate cultures and ideologies of workplace control.* Paper presented at the 83rd Annual Meeting of the American Sociological Association, San Francisco.

Lao Tzu. (1963). *The way of Lao Tzu* (Wing-Tsit, Trans.). Indianapolis, IN: Bobbs-Merrill. (Original work published 4th or 6th century B.C.)

McGregor, D. (1960). *The human side of enterprise.* New York: McGraw-Hill.

Ouchi, W. (1981). *Theory z*. Reading, MA: Addison-Wesley.
Pacanowsky, M., & O'Donnell-Trujillo, N. (1982). Communication and organizational cultures. *The Western Journal of Speech Communication, 46,* 115-130.
Peters, T., & Waterman, R. (1982). *In search of excellence*. New York: Harper & Row.
Sathe, V. (1985). *Culture and related corporate realities*. Homewood, IL: Richard D. Irwin.
Schein, E. (1992). *Organizational culture and leadership* (2nd ed.). San Francisco: Jossey-Bass.
Smircich, L., & Calás, M. (1987). Organizational culture: A critical assessment. In F. Jablin, L. Putnam, K. Roberts, & L. Porter (eds.), *Handbook of organizational communication* (pp. 228-263). Newbury Park, CA: Sage.

Sample Culture Assessment Test

Consider the following items. Choose the *one* response that most applies to your organization:

1. In this organization individuals are expected to give first priority to:
   A. Meeting the challenge of the individual task in which they are engaged.
   B. Co-operating with and attending to the needs of their fellow workers.
   C. Following the instructions of their superiors.
   D. Acting within the parameters of their job description.

2. The organization responds to its members as if they are:
   A. Associates or colleagues.
   B. Family or friends.
   C. Hired help.
   D. Contracted employees.

3. In this organization people are motivated and influenced most by:
   A. Their own commitment to the task.
   B. The respect and commitment that they have for their co-workers.
   C. The prospects of rewards or fear of punishment.
   D. The company policy or rule book.

4. A "good" employee is considered to be one who:
   A. Is self-motivated and willing to take risks and be innovative if the task demands it.
   B. Gets along well with other and is interested in their self-development.
   C. Always does what his/her boss tells him/her to do without question.
   D. Can be relied upon to stick to the company rules.

5. Relationships between work units or inter-departmentally are generally:
   A. Cooperative.
   B. Friendly.
   C. Competitive.
   D. Indifferent.

6. In this organization decisions tend to be:
   A. Made by the people on the spot who are close to the problem and have the appropriate task expertise.
   B. Made after considerable discussion and with the consensus of all those involved, regardless of their organizational hierarchy.
   C. Referred up the line to the person who has the most formal authority.
   D. Made by resort to established precedents.

7. It is most important for a new member of this organization to learn:
   A. To use his/her initiative to get the task completed.
   B. How to get on with his/her fellow workers.
   C. Who really counts in this organization and be aware of the political coalitions.
   D. The formal rules and regulations.

8. The dominant managerial style of this organization is:
   A. Democratic and open.
   B. Supportive and responsive to individual needs and idiosyncrasies.
   C. Authoritarian.
   D. Impersonal and remote.

If you scored mostly A's the dominant culture of your organization (as you perceive it) is "task/achievement"; mostly B's then "person/ support"; mostly C's then "power"; mostly D's then "role."

SOURCE: Cartwright and Cooper (1992, pp. 66-68).

NOTE: Reprinted by permission of Butterworth Heinmann Publishers, a division of Reed Educational & Professional Publishing Ltd.

Assessing and Changing Organizational Culture

Although most cultures are fairly deeply held and resistant to change, with careful attention cultures can and do change. This change can take many forms. A culture can be accentuated and its strength increased, it may be incrementally changed over rather lengthy periods of time, or it may be radically transformed usually over shorter periods of time. Each of these types of changes requires progressively more focused attention by organizational leaders or significant environmental changes—and often both—for transformational changes to occur.

Like any change in business strategy, cultural change can, and should, only be attempted with a clear plan and clear objectives. Before initiating a change process the organizational leader should be clear as to what the character of the existing culture is and what functions the existing culture performs. This requires careful assessment.

This chapter explores the reasons for initiating cultural change, the process of conducting an assessment of the culture, and the general features of change processes related to organizational cultures.

Key Objectives of the Chapter

▼ To identify situations where initiating a cultural change would be valuable

▼ To be able to perform a cultural assessment identifying the key characteristics of an existing culture and the need for a change

▼ To identify the arguments that convince particular others that a change is essential

▼ To recognize the primary sources of resistance to change

▼ To develop a change process through intervention in each of the places where culture is reproduced

▼ To produce an eight-step change plan

Questions to Consider

▼ Have you ever been involved in an organizational change effort? How did you feel? How did you respond? How did others respond? What might account for the differences in response you saw?

▼ What kinds of things could happen to an organization that would lead to a cultural change effort?

▼ Based on your own organizational experiences, to what extent do things have to change for management to want to give up its customary way of doing things?

▼ What kind of organizational changes might lead people to quit their organization?

▶ # Reasons for Initiating Cultural Change

> Culture is an asset that can also be a liability. It is an asset because culture eases and economizes communications, facilitates organizational decision making and control, and may generate higher levels of cooperation and commitment in the organization. The result is efficiency, in that these activities are accomplished with a lower expenditure of resources, such as time and money, than would otherwise be possible. The stronger the culture the greater the efficiency.
>
> Culture becomes a liability when important shared beliefs and values interfere with the needs of the business and of the company and the people who work for it. To the extent that the character of a company's culture leads its people to think and act in inappropriate ways, culture's efficiency will not help achieve effective results. This condition is usually a significant liability because it is hard to change a culture's content.
>
> —*Vijay Sathe (1985, p. 25)*

In the first chapter, several of the broader economic and social trends behind the interest in organizational culture were discussed. The positive aspects of assembling a business through building the corporate culture leads to an interest in guiding cultural changes. This section details motives for initiating cultural change.

Realizing the Competitive Advantage of a Strong Culture

Possibly the most important reason leaders have turned to managing culture is that a distinctive and strong corporate culture can give one business a competitive advantage over another in the same industry. High-performing companies need more than a competent workforce. For a company to be "excellent," it must also have a strong company spirit, a powerful corporate identity, and employees who hold a high level of organizational commitment and identification. This is especially true in service industries where the attitude of "frontline" personnel is the actual product being sold. To realize the competitive advantage of a strong culture, attention must be given to both the strength and the character of the culture.

Leaders properly work to strengthen the culture when they are happy with the character and they wish to increase the advantages that come with increased commitment and identification. Culture is profitable when it can increase competitiveness, facilitate organizational decision making and control, and generate higher levels of cooperation and commitment in the organization. Nevertheless, a strong culture can become a limitation when important shared beliefs and values interfere with the goals of the organization or members and the direction it needs to go to stay competitive. When a strong culture encourages people to think and act in ways that are inappropriate or not conducive to growth, a strong culture can actually hurt an organization or even lead to unethical behavior. Therefore, a strong culture may best be thought of as a balance between extremes. Managed effectively, a strong culture can lead to competitive advantage, but if the culture's character is wrong, a strong culture can lead to an organization's demise.

The competitive advantages of a strong culture often can only be realized by systematically working to change cultural character. This involves attempts to align values, assumptions, and common practices with business needs and environmental and regulatory changes. This is more difficult than changing the strength of a culture but is frequently much more important.

Building Employee Commitment, Identification, and Esprit de Corps

Managing culture may be most important when the company is experiencing difficulties with coordinating or motivating employees. This is frequently the case after business reorganizations or extensive leadership changes. In these situations both attitude and control problems may arise. A strong organizational culture can help redirect employee actions in a way that is less obtrusive and more participative yet more effective than bureaucratic rules and regulations. A strong set of values and beliefs can be more effective in shaping behavior than a long list of rules and regulations and direct supervisor intervention, especially when leader legitimacy is an issue.

A strong corporate spirit—an esprit de corps—plays a big part in motivating employees to work for collectively desired actions. When employees are highly committed to an organizational mission, they are more likely to go forward with actions that are consistent with company goals, even when these actions may not necessarily be in line with their individual or departmental priorities. When corporate philosophies saturate the organization in the form of a pervading culture, employees tend to identify more fully with the organization, resulting in increased commitment, organizational loyalty, and employee decisions that are in line with the organization's espoused mission.

Employee buy-in seems especially important in certain situations. For instance, when an organizational situation is complex and ambiguous, a set of common values and beliefs is extremely important as a regulatory mechanism. Ouchi (1981) refers to this as "clan control" and explains that subtle values sometimes cannot be put into words. A common understanding of organizational values among workers tends to prevent opportunistic behavior. This is especially true in our changing world of work when it is sometimes impossible for managers to "look over the shoulder" of and directly observe and manage employees. Today, effective management cannot merely consist of giving orders; it must focus on creating a shared vision and a sense of direction to people working in a company. The next three chapters focus on how leaders can generate organizational identification and increase buy-in among their employees in ways that respect employee needs and insights.

Employee Satisfaction

Employees are often more satisfied when they work in a "strong culture" company. This is not surprising. Part of the definition of a strong culture is shared values. Employees are happier when they feel as though they have a part in deciding and knowing corporate values and priorities. In addition, people have a natural inclination for wanting to belong to or identify with an organization. The opposite of identification is alienation. Without identification, employees are dead to the organization, a situation that leads to neither individual satisfaction nor organizational effectiveness.

Although a high level of satisfaction is important to all companies, it is especially important in knowledge-intensive and high-performance organizations. In these businesses, both the risks and costs of employee exit are great. In many high-end businesses, a significant part of company assets "go down the elevator every night." Such employees carry significant amounts of social and intellectual capital with them. Their organizational exit is often a competitor's gain. They often expect nontangible benefits from their place of work—such as stimulation, social relations, and excitement—that traditional manufacturing employees would have expected from their family and local communities.

Cultural Integration

The regular occurrences of mergers, acquisitions, and globalization efforts heighten the need to assess cultural compatibility and to integrate organizations that may be historically different. Toyota struggled and finally succeeded in bringing parts of its auto manufacturing to the United States; the AT&T/NCR merger never quite seemed to take; no one knows yet what will happen with Chrysler and Mercedes Benz or AT&T and TCI Cable.

To merge two or more organizations, move a department from one part of the world to another, or to acquire another organization, management must understand organizational culture. If the cultures of the two departments or organizations are completely different or are in conflict with one another, management may need to wage an extensive culture campaign or possibly rethink merging or moving the groups in the first place. Organizations should be assessed as more than instrumental constructions around business opportunities; they are flesh-and-blood entities made up of humans with distinct values and ways of working.

Due to rapid internationalization, interest in cross-cultural issues has increased dramatically. Some scholars argue about whether the organizational culture or national culture is more important when merging two or more organizations. Usually, it is best to perceive the two cultures as informing and constituting each other. In some situations, national culture is more important to an organizational decision, whereas in others, corporate culture has more to do with a course of action. Issues such as these are treated in more detail later.

Corporate Identity and Image

A strong culture, infused with expressive events and retold myths and stories, can be used to market the organization internally and externally. The cultural expression of corporate idiosyncrasies can become key elements in the organization's identity and image. As increasing numbers of marketing messages saturate the media and price wars become more and more common, a company can profit from creating a distinctive niche for itself in the eyes of consumers. It is no wonder, then, that businesses ranging from video rental shops and pizzerias to car washes and airlines have created "club" programs that invite "preferred consumers" to profit through returned business. When an organization has a strong culture, customers are no longer patrons; they are members, they are friends.

For instance, the Body Shop has used its focus on social responsibility to create employee identification and consumer commitment. The company has created a niche for itself in the cosmetics industry that many others have tried, but failed, to duplicate. Through a strong culture, Microsoft has also portrayed an image—both internally and externally—that it is at the pinnacle of computer software innovation. This image has attracted top technologically minded knowledge workers as well as millions of consumers.

Exercise 2.1

Visualize what you would desire in a culture for an "ideal" organization. How would people feel about the company? How would they treat work? What values would be most central? How would management act in such an environment?

▶ Evaluating a Particular Culture

Many reasons exist for working to change a corporate culture. But change without careful assessment is usually misguided. Carefully examining an organization's culture provides a richer understanding of how organizations really work, uncovers the strengths and weaknesses, and shows where and why resistance to change is likely. On the basis of such assessment a clearer determination can be made regarding whether a cultural change is necessary.

Assessing the Nature of a Culture

Assessing a culture is complex and difficult. Internalized beliefs, assumptions, and values cannot be easily observed or measured. Similar values and decisional premises embedded in common routines and practices are difficult to infer in any simple way.

Researchers have developed many methods for deciphering culture. Most take significant lengths of time and are usually best done by trained outside experts. Schein (1992) provides well the details of systematic analysis, including both the type of commitment needed in the company itself and the process of study. The analysis of culture requires multiple methods of studying the variety of ways culture is produced and reproduced in organizational life. Here are a number of elements of organizational life of interest in assessment:

Employee feelings of involvement, identification, and commitment

Vocabulary and metaphors used in discussing organizational events

Stories, myths, legends

Rites and rituals

Routines of decision making and handling problems

Types and processes of conflict

Physical layout of the business

Espoused values in company documents

Company histories

Socialization processes

Strategies of justification

Emotional expression and tone

In exploring these elements observers must ask questions, make observations, read documents, and trust their gut feelings. Initially, an observer must try to understand the world as understood by organizational members. But ultimately, the observer must infer the more deeply held ways of seeing and thinking about the world and the values and assumptions used in making decisions and judgments in it. Only with this type of insight can change engage the more fundamental aspect of culture and its impact in the organization.

A number of self-administered cultural analyses are also possible. Generally, the understanding gathered from these is not as rich but may still provide useful insights. Repertory grids and focus group discussions have both been used with some success. Perhaps the easiest to administer and most sensitive instrument is based on the 20-statement test.

With this test organizational members are asked to anonymously write 20 statements completing the phrase, "My department (organization) is . . ." Members are asked to write these as if they were writing to themselves and to put them in the order as they occur, not reflecting on importance. Q-sorts or other forms of theme analysis can be used to fairly quickly tap into basic shared perspectives. After that it is usually not too hard to infer basic values and assumptions (see Locatelli & West, 1996).

Exercise 2.2

Complete a 20-statement test for your own culture. Identify three themes that characterize the culture (themes that would sum it up for an outsider). What are the everyday life events, structures, stories, and activities that you would use as evidence for the descriptive statements you made?

Determining That a Cultural Change Is Needed

Many types of cultural changes may be desired. Generally, these aim at changing either the character or the strength of the culture. Of the two, changing the strength requires much less effort. Character changes are much more difficult. Whenever possible a character change should be accomplished slowly through the gradual development of relationships between the existing culture and new perspectives and ways of thinking. In some cases a major transformation is desired. Usually, these are a result of a major transition in the organization or environmental or regulatory change. In these cases more attention must be given to demonstrating the need for change, justifications for interventions, and consequences for failing to change.

Changing the Culture's Strength. The general corporate culture may be well aligned with business objectives but still not generate the type of intensity desired. In these cases the attempt needs to clarify the existing values and culturally based activities and work to extend them to new arenas and get more people to buy in more completely. This may require intervention in nonsupportive subcultures and providing more activities that highlight and celebrate positive cultural elements.

Recall, however, that strong cultures are not always positive, even when they support business objectives. If innovation is important or the business environment is fairly turbulent, the weaker culture provides opportunity for planned diversity and the ability to foresee and respond to changes.

Changing the Culture's Character. Cultural character needs to be changed when the dominant culture promotes behaviors that are inconsistent with business needs and member relations. Compliance with objectives may be very weak in such cases. The need to change the culture's character is most pressing when other means of monitoring and directing behavior are especially costly or difficult.

Since changing cultural character is difficult, careful evaluation of the existing culture is important. With creativity desired results often can be achieved by methods of behavioral change or through extension and adaptation of the existing culture. In the case of a major upheaval in the business environment, one must reasonably ask whether sufficient time is available for a transformation of the culture or whether less enduring but more rapid changes or temporary arrangements are possible.

▶ Leading the Cultural Change

Intentional culture change efforts, like any change, begins with a strategy. The strategy reflects both a desired future state and a process for getting there. Generally, in today's complex business situations the desired future state of affairs has to be clear and compelling but sufficiently ambiguous and adaptable that the company can learn during the change process, seize emergent opportunities, and be ready to recognize that futures look different when you get there. Positive direction can be given that still allows space for specific interpretations and employees adding their own meaning. This will be explored further when vision statements are discussed.

Here the attention will be directed to the process of change. Discussion includes the motivation for and resistance to cultural change, where leaders can intervene in normal cultural reproductive processes to create change, and steps to achieve a major cultural transformation.

Motivation for Cultural Change

Motivation for change can be intrinsic, extrinsic, or both. Intrinsic motivation for change tends to be highest when the present culture is weak and organizational members genuinely feel change is needed. Usually, people only feel the need for a change when there is clear and undeniable evidence that organizational survival and people's chances for success are at stake. When the existing culture is strong, such a need must be established and felt within existing values and assumptions. This is difficult, since it is often those same values and perspectives that kept organizational members from perceiving the need earlier on. Establishing need is critical to internal motivation. With a weaker culture, mere demonstration of the advantage of a new way of approaching problems may be sufficient.

External motivation may be provided through a variety of traditional inducements. Reward systems can be developed that advantage new ways of handling organizational choices. Change in such systems often can have far more influence than espousing and justifying new values, especially if the values are advocated without tangible rewards for acceptance. Symbolic inducements can also be used, visibly providing acknowledgment and advantages to those more allegiant to the new cultural principles.

Resistance to Cultural Change

Business leaders rarely anticipate the extent of the resistance to planned changes. One reason for this is that the leaders have had more time to think about the change and more fully understand the reasons for it. But equally important, leaders often have less to lose from it. It is their plan; they are protected in it. Employees, on the other hand, are often surprised, do not understand the reasoning, did not participate in the choice, and see themselves as having much to lose. Overcoming these differences between leaders and other members is possible, as discussed below and in later chapters. Essentially, fuller communication, participation in choice and implementation, trust, and genuine protection reduce resistance.

Most leaders enter change efforts motivated and even excited. The change is fresh and new for them, but many employees have a different experiential history. Often, they have been reorganized and developed to death. They have been through every change effort imaginable. They are understandably cynical. They know most are talk and are rarely carried through. Employees hear change as more work without more pay—work that rarely makes a difference, advocated by people who do not know what their job requires. They have developed a system of shortcuts and standard expectations that have given them efficiency and a measure of autonomy. At least temporarily, all that will go away. For a while the rules will be up for grabs. They have learned to play along without making real change until the next management initiative comes along and removes the need.

To a large extent, the leader has no choice but to try to make this change effort different, a claim all employees have heard before. In a sense, the leader has to really, really mean it this time (Can Lucy get Charlie Brown to try to kick the football one more time?) and make it real.

Furthermore, most resistance is unintentional. Old habits and automatic responses are hard to recognize and change. The deeper the changes, the more likely they will enter realms of life invisible to employees. As with riding a bicycle, one's early learnings never quite go away. Most people carry about thousands of social recipes for handling routine life events. They have used these over and over again for most of their lives. And most have worked reasonably well or they would have gone away some time ago. When ways of responding become entrenched, even repeated failure rarely leads to change. Many people assume if they just do what they usually do only with more strength and tenacity they will succeed. Only focused attention can make these automatic response patterns visible, let alone provide a motivation to change.

Finally, fear is a key element in most resistance. Some fears are well founded and some are not. Most can be reduced by taking into account the sources of the fear and reducing the potential negative impact on employees.

The most basic fear is the fear of the unknown. Employees reasonably ask what the new culture will look like. Are they likely to be able to succeed in it? How will the rules change? They fear failure. Even, or perhaps especially, the most successful can reasonably question whether they will enjoy the same levels of success. New cultures lead to the possibility of embarrassment and awkwardness in learning and handling situations. And employees fear possible rejection by those still advancing the old culture and by those working in the new.

These fears are exacerbated by a sense of the loss of control. One is not just entering the unknown, one is entering it as a changing person who does not know fully how he or she will respond in the new situation or even what he or she will be. Fears can be reduced by providing time, protection, information, and personal control.

Exercise 2.3

During a family Thanksgiving dinner, one of us asked a cousin how things were going at work. The cousin replied with rolled eyes that the company's management had started this new program. They wanted to empower people and a lot more of the decisions would be made in teams. Mostly, no one knew what they were doing and it was taking a lot of extra time. He was not sure what they wanted from him but knew that new systems of accountability were going to be in place. He was doing a lot of guessing and felt that his skills were not being used well. Most people like him had assumed that personnel would be cut along the way, and he just hoped to ride this out until management came up with another new idea.

* Why do you think that this new program was met with this type of reaction?
* What might management have done to make this less likely?
* Have you ever felt like the cousin?
* What is the piece of this that the cousin seems to have missed?
* What are the values the cousin appears to hold? How could these be brought into a relation to the new program?
* What would you do now if you were a manager of this company and had overheard this story?
* Recall a time when your unit was reorganized, you were asked to make a significant change in your way of working, or your job requirements were altered. What did you fear most in making the change? What most motivated you to stick with it? In what ways did you resist the change, if any? Why might others respond to similar events differently?

▶ The Change Process

Despite the difficulties of change, change does happen. Change is possible partly as a function of the nature of culture itself. Culture does not reside somewhere like a balloon or building; it must be constantly reproduced in the activities of people. As shown earlier, culture is better thought of as the reoccurrence of specific meanings, personal identities, and activities than as the cause of them. Culture is an endless negotiation by organizational members. Activities and interactions are part of the development of shared interpretations and common assumptions.

Intervention in Cultural Reproductive Processes

Culture is reproduced in a number of organizational processes. These processes include at the minimum (a) hiring and new member training; (b) the advocacy of values, principles, and visions and the telling of stories; (c) the justification of choices through reason giving, accounts, and explanations; (d) the physical artifacts, nature of the work process and performance appraisals, and decisional routines; and, finally, (e) the systematic defection or removal of employees from the unit or organization. Intervention is possible in each, or better all, of these processes.

1. Systematically hiring employees who already share the desired cultural qualities is often easier than changing older employees. Such a choice should be done with care to ensure the adequate diversity and variety necessary for innovation, organizational learning, and adaptation to a changing environment. Early socialization processes are often more lasting than later interventions.

2. Chapters 3 and 4 look much more closely at explicit "cultural communication" through value advocacy, storytelling, and visions. Clearly, as shown later, leaders must "walk the talk," but they must also clearly "talk the talk."

3. All reason giving, accounts, and justifications carry implicit values and assumptions. During normal processes of cultural reproduction, the values and assumption remain invisible. Only occasionally will an activity appear so lacking in sense that explicit questions of values and as-

sumptions are raised. Such communicative acts may be rare, since the members fill in the reasoning on their own. As cultures change, uncertainty and ambiguity increase. Questions like "What was meant by that?" or "Why was that done?" become more common. And it is increasingly likely that organizational members will provide their own explanations that may be quite different from those that organizational leaders desire. Activities and events needing explanation provide an excellent opportunity for leaders to direct member interpretive processes.

4. Culture is reproduced through the physical arrangements of offices and the innumerable ways that day-to-day work and decisions are handled. Values are more convincingly communicated through actions than through words. This is not to diminish the effective use of words. Actions are always subject to interpretations, words frame interpretations, and interpretations influence cultural reproductions. But creating clear behavioral objectives desired in the new culture and providing good measures for achievement are critical to the new culture's development. Try investigating standard practices everywhere to assess the ways they hinder or support the new culture. Culture will not change if reward systems and decision-making practices stay the same.

5. Inevitably, some employees cannot or do not wish to be part of a new culture. Old cultures disappear partly from the voluntary or encouraged departure of these employees. Cultural change is helped by systematic procedures for early retirement, transferring, or other means of removal.

Steps to Achieve a Major Transformation

John Kotter (1995), a professor in the Harvard Business School and major contributor to understanding change processes, suggests an eight-step process to achieving a major transformation in a business. Most of these are relevant to more minor attempts to shape culture.

Establish a Sense of Urgency. As already indicated, internal motivation to change is based on a clear understanding of threatening external conditions or competitive advantage to be gained. Evidence for a crisis, potential crisis, or major opportunity must be presented clearly to the members who are asked to change or the aggressive cooperation necessary for change will not occur.

Kotter (1995) estimates that over 50% of all change efforts fail because of the lack of felt urgency. The type of evidence necessary to be convincing is heavily dependent on past experiences of personnel and the existing culture. For example, members of a paper company who are used to wide market fluctuations in pulp paper prices are not likely to be motivated by an extreme one-quarter loss. Many managers prefer to give orders rather than collect and distribute evidence. They are not likely to lead change efforts.

Urgency also suggests moving fast. Change should be initiated on all fronts at the start with phase-in coordinated in a timely fashion. Slow changes are not more comfortable. They often allow resistance to consolidate and contradictions to exist in the company. Fast changes do not mean that care cannot be taken to understand fears and provide meaningful transitions. But these should be anticipated and planned for from the very outset. Response should not wait for actual presence of a problem.

Form a Powerful Guiding Coalition. Change processes of all sorts across different aspects of life are usually lead by a cluster of early adopters who become critical parts of the diffusion to others. Organizational change is little different. It is not sufficient for upper management or the upper management team alone to support a change. Early adopters exist throughout most organizations. Others watch them for ideas and how they are treated. As T. J. and Sandar Larkin (1996) have shown convincingly, frontline supervisors are especially important to change efforts.

A change team has to be developed that is sufficiently diverse, motivated and powerful to influence the variety of people to be effected in the change process. If the team members can work together, they can also learn from and give support to each other, especially during the early months. Retreats and other activities can aid this group in preparing for the opposition it eventually will face.

Create a Guiding Vision. Plans and directives lack force unless accompanied by a clear and easily understood vision. The urgency of change can create diminished motivation and even exit by key members if not matched by a compelling notion of what can be. Important qualities of visions are the focus of the next chapter.

Communicate the Vision. A vision without the voice of a prophet can neither inspire nor guide. Visions are often undercommunicated and communicated in an ineffective manner. Undercommunication usually occurs when the vision remains a property of upper managers. They may be clear about where they are going, but the various instructions and directives they send out do not carry the vision. These often make little sense and fail to inspire. The larger the change, the greater the need is to explain and demonstrate at every possible occasion.

Poor communication occurs when upper managers preach the values but do little to get directly involved in the change effort. The negative effect is compounded when management actually continues to operate in ways that contradict the new vision. Videos, email, publications, coffee cups, and large meetings rarely help. Communication should be face to face whenever possible. Presentations and publications should contain facts and analyses rather than slogans. Meetings should answer real questions rather than be used to spin the line. A vision needs to be written into the day-to-day interactions. Rewriting policy materials and appraisal processes presents a new vision much more clearly and honestly than posters.

Furthermore, as discussed later, a presentation is not communication. Communication takes two—one to have meaning and send a message and another to hear it and decide what it means. People respond to the vision that they hear, not the one that was meant. An upper manager's vision to increase customer satisfaction can be heard by the supervisor as another job to add on top of an already heavy workload and having to change several work processes to customize products for different customers. The heard vision is hardly inspirational. People reasonably ask, "What's in it for me?" A well-articulated vision must provide a way for employees to answer that positively. Generalized values and slogans rarely do that.

Empower Others to Act. Often managers try to overmanage change. They want to control everything. But change processes are very complex. No one can orchestrate the process all the way. Furthermore, change requires an internal change by organizational members. Internal changes do not happen by people being told or required to comply. People must embrace such changes for themselves, make them their own. People model their changes on others they perceive to be similar to themselves. They must be enabled to make the vision over as their own within the broad parameters for coordination. Get people involved as soon as possible. Trying things out that succeed provides encouragement for further change.

Once a positive process gets going, the most that upper management can do is simply not let things get in the way. This requires removing obstacles to change. Job categories and standard work expectations often continue to undermine the vision. Changing hearts, minds, and souls cannot be sustained when people are put back into the same constraints. Appraisal and other systems or structures need to be changed when they work against the vision. And finally, upper management has to encourage risk taking and remove penalties for failure in the short term as new things are tried out.

Create Small Wins Along the Way. Cultural change is a slow process even when aggressively pursued. Initially, one might even expect lower morale and some decline in performance. Significant changes, even when positive, disrupt easy automatic processes. As an analogy, learning to dribble a basketball with the left hand may be frustrating for a right-handed person, even if he or she knows that no serious player can play with the right hand alone.

An important way to avoid frustration and loss of momentum is to build in small wins that can be shared and celebrated. Try to imagine a significant weight loss program or fitness program without reoccurring measurements that show progress that can be shared with others. Especially the guiding coalition will need progress checks and means of celebrating accomplishment. Coalition members will need it for themselves, and others will be watching.

Consolidate Improvements and Create More Change. Even the best change effort grows tiring after a couple of years. It is to be hoped that some success has been achieved by this time and people have other things to attend to. It is easy to think that the process is done or can be put on the back burner. This is usually a mistake.

Resistance usually resides under the surface for some time waiting for the opportunity to return. Many in the company may still be imitating the new without having internalized it. It is amazing how quickly some people revert to old patterns the first time a crisis hits. And all changes gradually become routinized in ways that obscure the vision. The prophets often become priests. Ideally, a leader of a change effort can consolidate small wins and use them as a basis to go after even more entrenched structures and perspectives. Changes in process can truly become changes in deeply held values, but that takes years.

Institutionalize the New Culture. Without a grounding in everyday routines and members' value systems, all changes in attitudes and ways of talking will gradually pass away. Change efforts are often connected to charismatic leaders. When they leave, only firmly grounded changes will remain. As conditions of urgency now seem at bay, motivation for continued improvement may wane. People continue to need to be shown how the change really made the performance difference. And new managers need to be selected that will continue to champion the vision and the cultural changes needed.

Exercise 2.4

Recall your vision of a positive culture for an organization of which you are a part. Sketch how you would accomplish each of Kotter's (1995) eight steps.

▶ Review Questions

▼ When would an explicit cultural change process be most valuable?

▼ What are some of the things you would look at when trying to determine the character of a particular culture?

▼ What might you do to enhance the strength of an organization's culture?

▼ When might a strong culture be a problem?

▼ What factors influence the internal motivation of organizational members to engage in a cultural change?

▼ Why might employees fear and resist a cultural change effort?

▼ What are the sites of cultural reproduction? How can you intervene in each?

▼ Why is a sense of urgency important in initiating a cultural change process?

▼ If you were building a guiding coalition for the change effort, how would you induce or enroll members?

▼ What is the best way to express the vision for change?

Discussion Questions

▼ In your organization, which organizational members have been most accepting of change? Why do you think they are different from others?

▼ What are the leading forms of resistance to change in your organization? What types of messages would most likely reduce the resistance?

▼ What do you think of Kotter's (1995) eight steps to change? From your experience, which have been least followed?

▼ When a change process was attempted in an organization of which you were a part, how successful was it? Where did it most succeed and most fail? What might you do differently now?

References and Recommended Readings

Kotter, J. P. (1995, March-April). Leading change: Why transformation efforts fail. *Harvard Business Review*, pp. 59-67.

Larkin, T. J., & Larkin, S. (1996, May-June). Reaching and changing frontline employees. *Harvard Business Review*, pp. 95-104.

Liedtka, J., & Rosenblum, J. (1996). Shaping conversations: Making strategy, managing change. *California Management Review, 39*, 141-157.

Locatelli, V., & West, M. (1996). On elephants and blind researchers: Methods for assessing culture in organizations. *Leadership & Organization Development Journal, 17*, 12-21.

Nutt, P., & Backoff, R. (1997). Organizational transformation. *Journal of Management Inquiry, 6*, 235-254.

Ouchi, W. (1981). *Theory Z*. Reading, MA: Addison-Wesley.

Sathe, V. (1985). *Culture and related corporate realities*. Homewood, IL: Richard D. Irwin.

Schein, E. (1992). *Organizational culture and leadership* (2nd ed.). San Francisco: Jossey-Bass.

Schoenberger, E. (1997). *The cultural crisis of the firm*. Oxford, UK: Blackwell.

Vision and Cultural Development

Developing and acting on a strong vision is vital to an organization. Vision is one of the key elements that distinguish a manager from a leader. To be effective, however, a vision statement must be collaboratively constructed and "owned" by members across organizational levels. Unless the vision is clearly communicated and integrated into organizational practices, it is likely to have little effect. No matter how often strategic plans are revised and mission statements revisited, without a strong commitment to these guiding principles they cannot strengthen an organization. This chapter outlines what a vision is and shows how some of the world's premier organizations have turned a commitment to a strong vision into unparalleled success.

To be useful, a vision statement must be integrated with the cultural value systems of the organization. The path toward vision achievement must be followed every day and enacted in routine interactions and communication. Vision helps build identification with the core purpose of the organization, and identification gives employees a sense of accomplishment in the work that they do, which in turn drives them to strive toward accomplishment of organizational and member objectives. A strong, shared vision is good for the organization at all levels.

Key Objectives of the Chapter

▼ To explain the importance of a long-term vision

▼ To illustrate how to develop a powerful vision statement

▼ To explore means of reinforcing culture and building employee identification

▼ To help in the building of shared visions

▼ To provide a rationale for involving organizational members in developing and implementing a shared vision

Questions to Consider

▼ Think of an organization of which you are a member. This may be a workplace or corporate organization, but might also be a student organization, religious group, sports team, or community service organization. Wherever people "organize" their activity through communication, organizational work is being done. Does this organization have a clearly articulated vision?

▼ What are its core values?

▼ What is the value of the product or service that it produces or provides?

▼ Are organizational members strongly identified with the organization? Why? Why not?

▼ What can you do to ensure that the daily operations move the organization toward fulfillment of its vision?

Building a Vision

Unless company objectives are in harmony with your [employee] objectives, unless our corporate way of life is compatible with the way you want to work and what you want to achieve, there is no way we can succeed, no chance to excel. But how do we make sure the goals of the corporation are consistent with the goals of our employees? How can we get everyone working together to push this company out front? The answer is simple. Start talking. Define the rules by which we will play the game. Start talking about our philosophy. Write it down, criticize it, change it if it needs changing. Then let it stand out there so we can be measured and challenged to make it even better.
—*Joseph D. Williams, CEO, Warner-Lambert*
(quoted by Hebert in Goodman [1998] p. 73)

Most organizations have a mission statement that articulates the overall purpose that the organization was founded to accomplish. Such a statement is generally contained in the governing documents of the organization, such as a constitution, bylaws, policy manuals, or employee handbooks. It may also be communicated informally through stories that articulate "what we are about here." A mission statement generally reflects what the founders of the organization hoped to accomplish when it was created.

Similarly, many corporate organizations spend a great deal of time and money on meetings aimed at strategic planning. These sessions are frequently designed to identify what the organization is currently doing and what are its strengths and weaknesses. A strategic plan generally outlines how the organization intends to fulfill its mission.

Although each of these elements is related to the development of an organizational vision, they differ from each other. A mission tells you where the organization wants to go; the strategic plan tells you how it intends to get there. A vision, however, helps you see the importance of getting where you want to go and understand why some paths there are better suited to some organizations than others.

Since most organizations perform a multitude of different tasks to arrive at their end goal or product, a vision can also serve a coordinating function. It can provide a framework that allows organizational members to make sense of the particular tasks that they are responsible for performing in the context of the larger purpose of the organization. In this way the vision helps contextualize the purpose of everything that gets done in an organization. The vision inspires, motivates, and creates a sense of purpose that organizational members can buy into.

In short, a good vision is realistic enough to create a recognizable picture of the future, powerful enough to generate commitment to performance, coherent enough to provide coordination, and open enough that others can make it over into their own. If this is done the vision can inspire and motivate, provide direction, and enable benchmarking of progress toward the future.

Exercise 3.1

● Richard Allen (1995) suggested a vision is formed by asking basic questions. Address each of these in relationship to an organization that you belong to:

- What is our purpose?
- What is our driving force?
- What are our core values?
- What do we do best?
- What do we want to accomplish?
- What do we want to change?

● Articulate your vision for your organization. Is the current culture conducive to achieving it?

● How might others' visions for the organization differ?

▶ Why a Long-Term Vision?

A vision is always just out of reach. It gives organizational members something to strive for. As such, a clear vision statement must be future focused. By developing a clear sense of where you want to go, you move the organization beyond immediate preoccupations with product design, time to market, and even staying ahead of the competition. By focusing down the road, day-to-day challenges can be addressed in the context of whether they move the organization toward its goal.

Organizations that set the standard by which others measure themselves do so by focusing more on where they want to go than on where their competition is going. This is not to say that an awareness of current circumstances or markets is not important. What this does mean, though, is that as long as your goal is to stay ahead of the pack, you are only measuring yourself against that pack. Companies that follow those principles may be successful. They may even make a great deal of money. They are unlikely to be trendsetters, however.

There is a good reason that CEOs like Bill Gates, Steve Jobs, Lee Iacocca, Sam Walton, and even Walt Disney were considered *visionary*. Gates still runs Microsoft with the goal of "putting a computer on every desk, and in every home, all running Microsoft software" (quoted in Lewis, 1997, p. 10). This vision says little about how day-to-day operations are conducted, but this guiding principle is part of what helps determine how changing market conditions are responded to.

When an organization has a clear sense of purpose and knows where it wants to go, that gives meaning to what happens day in and day out and helps avoid common "process-improvement" pitfalls. Total quality management (TQM), quality circles, teaming, and benchmarking, among countless other trendy activities for organizational improvement, will repeatedly fall short of their goal, as long as process is examined devoid of context. A strong long-term vision gives cohesion to the work of an organization. With this sense of purpose in mind, quality improvement takes on new life.

Qualities of a Strong Vision

In an organization with strong vision, quality improvement is not something that only takes place when market share drops or when serious problems are identified. Organizations with a strong vision consistently rise to the challenge of outdoing themselves. This is not to say that they do not recognize or reward successes, but rather that each success is viewed as a milestone along the route to fulfilling a larger purpose. Although every organization must set its own vision and develop its own standards, there are certain characteristics that can provide guidelines for thinking about an organization's vision.

The Vision Provides a Sense of Direction for Organizations

A vision articulates where the organization is headed and what it is trying to accomplish. A vision projects an exciting future and is realistic. It is a direction toward the future based in both possibilities and desire. Things like a 5-year plan may help provide focus and give some sense of direction, but a task-oriented plan is not a vision. The vision clearly takes into account the cultural values of the organization and articulates what the organization aims to achieve. The day-to-day performance objectives at Microsoft may vary widely, but the long-term vision continues to guide the organization forward.

A Clear Vision Provides a Context for Decision Making

Although a long-term vision may not be about day-to-day decisions, it does help to shape and guide them. A vision statement should be the backdrop against which all choices and decisions can be measured and assessed. Many good and interesting ideas emerge in a market environment. Successful organizations are able to choose between them and act on only those that move them toward the accomplishment of their vision.

At Ford, the vision of "Quality is Job 1" allows managers and executives to make clear-cut decisions about product models. Increased performance or sleeker body designs are considered if they collectively contribute to creating a higher quality product. Alone, they do not serve the goals of the organization. When important decisions have to be made, an organization with a clear vision of its future can ask, "Will this help us accomplish our goals?" "Does this move us in the direction we have committed to follow?"

A Shared Vision Must Reflect Organizational Values and Culture

For a vision to serve its function and guide the organization surely forward, it must be believed and acted on by members at all levels of the organization. For this to occur, the organizational mission and the day-to-day culture and practices of the organization must be well matched. A vision for the future of an organization must arise out of its present circumstances. The cultural framework in which organizational members make sense of their work experience must be attended to in the process of developing a vision for the organization's future.

As the vision aims to move the organization forward and prepares it for change, it must also provide a sense of direction and give focus for organizational members. At the same time that the articulation of a vision should take these concerns into consideration, the ultimate implementation of processes to achieve the vision must be congruent with what members are being told. If the messages that they hear in training seminars and read in company documents do not reflect members' daily experience, not only are they less likely to be motivated to work toward fulfillment of the organizational vision, they are more likely to be distrustful of management. Obviously, neither of these conditions leads the organization in a positive direction.

The vision-culture link can be thought of as cyclical in nature, with the vision both arising out of the larger organizational culture and helping to shape and focus the evolution of that culture. The time during which the organizational vision is defined is a good time to assess the nature of the organizational culture. If the culture is not conducive to carrying out the vision of the organization, changes may be required at other levels.

Throughout this process it is important to keep in mind that organizational members often have a significant amount of themselves invested in the day-to-day routines and practices of the organization. Making sweeping changes without their input is likely to lead to dissatisfaction and alienation, not to increased identification. This is another reason why it is so important for the organizational vision to be co-constructed by members all across the organization.

A Clear Vision Recognizes and Responds to a Pressing Need

For organizational members to feel that their efforts are useful and meaningful, the product or service that the organization is committed to providing must meet a need that is both real and perceived. Federal Express is a prime example of an organization that was founded and has thrived on the continuous fulfillment of a felt need. When first founded, the company recognized the difficulties faced by organizations in which the members could converse and reach agreements very rapidly by electronic means of communication but were then often forced to wait several days for the delivery of official documents that would allow them to finalize agreements already reached informally.

The company was founded with a vision of providing guaranteed overnight delivery of letters and small parcels. To achieve this ambitious goal, it built in quality control measures very early on that would both provide accountability and allow organizational members to see the effects of their success more readily. Allowing customers to call or use computer software to easily track their shipments increased organizational members' incentives to ensure that the vision of the organization was fulfilled. It also allowed members to more easily observe how their contributions helped to meet real needs by fulfilling the vision of the company.

A Vision Helps Create a Strong Future by Acting in the Present

Although the function of a vision is to enable the organization to focus on the big picture and see a future for itself, knowing where one is headed allows one to take decisive action in the present to move in that direction. Being future focused will not help the organization to move forward unless steps are taken every day to move in that direction.

Managers become leaders when they are able to enact the values and principles embedded in the organizational vision in their day-to-day interactions with employees and in the approach that they take to their own job performance. Once a vision for the organization has been articulated, it must become an integral part of day-to-day routines for it to lead to increased identification or play a significant role in shaping the future of the organization. It is the responsibility of individuals in leadership positions to communicate the vision.

This involves more than managers' reciting the organization's vision statement to their subordinates, however. Sometimes understanding at a deeper level what the accomplishment of that vision involves and using that framework to shape everything from job descriptions to performance evaluations can have a more powerful impact. Conveying the underlying goals that the vision aims to accomplish is what will ultimately help shape the direction of the organization.

Many companies have invested a great deal of time and energy in the development of mission statements and the articulation of a vision. Far too frequently, however, the outcome of the planning stage gets carefully written up into policy manuals or annual reports without ever having a significant impact on the day-to-day operations of the organization. This is not a vision. This does not lead to inspiration. This does not strengthen organizational culture or enhance member identification. This is an expensive way to spend a great deal of time and money while accomplishing little, if anything, of any real value to the organization.

If, however, a vision is used to help coordinate the activities of subcultural groups within the larger organization, it can have a powerful unifying effect. A vision cannot be applied uniformly across subunits in a corporation in most cases. For this reason, developing that underlying sense of where the vision is directing the organization and being able to help members across the organizational system see the relevance of its focus to their functions can often be more helpful than any number of formal seminars or campaigns for increasing the commitment of multiple organizational members to the future direction of the organizational system.

How Do These Characteristics Combine to Create Strong Vision?

We have seen that to create a shared vision, the vision must provide an overall aim or direction for the organization. In doing so, as the vision shapes the way the organization thinks about its future it also guides the choices that are made about how to act today. For this to lead to increased employee identification, the vision must reflect organizational values. If it does not, members are less likely to be highly identified with the organization and more likely to be skeptical of management.

When a true, shared vision is developed, organizational members have something to believe in and feel a sense of purpose in their work. It is this belief that the work that they do serves a purpose and has meaning that leads employees to develop a strong identification with the mission of the organization and take action to help accomplish it. They are increasingly encouraged to do so to the extent that the product or service provided and the overall aim of the vision respond to a real and pressing need.

All of these factors must be complemented by day-to-day enactment of the values and principles articulated in the vision. This daily enactment involves the clear communication of the broader sense of vision to organizational members. A vision statement does little good on a shelf or even on a wall. Simply reciting the vision statement without accompanying action is not sufficient either. Leaders must "walk the talk" and demonstrate their continued and unwavering commitment to fulfilling the organizational vision. Unwavering does not mean unquestioning, however, and successful organizations regularly assess the extent to which their vision responds to the changing needs of the environment.

▶ Adapting to Change

We have already mentioned that to remain successful, an organization must remain flexible and adaptive to change. It is important to recognize, too, however, that even the most well intended visions can turn out to have been misguided or not lead the organization in productive directions. The wisest leaders expect to encounter failures on the road to success. Although difficulties are never exactly welcomed, leaders with a strong vision for the organization are able to look at failures and mistakes as opportunities for unparalleled learning and organizational growth. Sometimes mistakes are able to provide us with insights and point us in directions that would have been invisible otherwise.

Visions are about recognizing the opportunities in setbacks and rising to meet new challenges. Those who see errors as someone's fault typically spend valuable time reorganizing human resources, without ever fundamentally altering the circumstances that led to the negative outcome in the first place. Those who are able to see obstacles as the by-product of poor planning, of misguided vision, or of unforeseen circumstances are better able to make rapid reassessments and use temporary setbacks to catapult the organization more surely toward a more desirable outcome. For these changes in direction to take place, however, it is critical that leaders secure the support of organizational members, for they are the ones who will be responsible for the daily activities that move the organization in particular directions.

▶ Building Identification

What exactly does building identification entail? What is an "identified" employee? How does building identification both strengthen the organization and enhance the work experience for organizational members?

Building identification involves developing systems in which organizational members are inspired, encouraged, and motivated to take action. An identified employee is one who shares core values with the mission of the organization and feels a sense of gratification and accomplishment by helping to achieve organizational objectives. Such identified individuals help build a strong organization, because those that work there are committed to achieving the overall goals that it seeks to accomplish.

When employees identify with an organizational vision, they feel increased degrees of satisfaction from the performance of tasks when they are able to see how their work helps to create an outcome of which they are supportive. A clearly articulated vision and the incorporation of its underlying principles into daily activities may help to create the necessary conditions for identification, but unless members take personal ownership of the process of achieving the goals of the organization, such identification will be tenuous at best. For an organizational member to develop a deeper sense of commitment to the organizational project, Paul Strebel (1996) suggests that they must be able to answer questions such as

▼ What is my role in achieving the goals of the organization?

▼ How does my job or role fit into the bigger picture?

▼ How will my task performance be supported by the organization (materially, financially?)

▼ What forms of assessment will be available to help me gage my contributions?

▼ How is my compensation related to my performance of organizational objectives?

Although many of these questions are typically answered in policy and procedure manuals, having such questions answered personally on a case-by-case basis may lend greater support to the project. The development of individual agreements with organizational members can provide an opportunity to clarify explicitly how the tasks performed by particular organizational members help to move the organization in a desired direction. This can be beneficial both to employees/members and to management.

Employees may develop a deeper sense of the importance of their job to the organization and feel more compelled to help the organization achieve its mission. This can be both intrinsically and extrinsically rewarding. From a managerial perspective, developing a deeper sense of the importance of the many interrelated tasks that must be performed to achieve objectives may be useful later on in making decisions about organizational change. Entering into such a process creates an environment in which employees are encouraged and inspired to engage in innovative activity that helps move the organization toward its desired goals and then sets up a reward structure for recognizing the contributions that are ultimately made.

Exercise 3.2

- What leads members to identify with an organization? What increases and lessens the strength of identification?

- Complete the sample organization identification questionnaire at the end of the chapter (Appendix 3.1). How might organizational culture be managed to increase identification?

▶ Developing and Implementing a Vision

For an organizational leader or someone who may find himself or herself in a leadership role in the future, understanding how to develop and implement vision in an organization is an important skill. Once you understand the importance of shared vision, are able to see its connection to the strength of an organization's culture, and have identified the key players in the process, you must devise a strategy for facilitating the development of this vision. The following steps provide a general overview of what to do in the process of creating a vision. As with any activity of this importance to an organization, however, enlisting the assistance of trained professionals is important to the success of this endeavor.

The Importance of a Qualified Facilitator

Having an individual or small team of individuals who can assist in the structuring of the visioning process is critical to its success. This individual should have a relatively small stake in the outcome of the visioning process in order to be better able to act in such a way as to encourage the representation of a broad range of perspectives and challenge the status quo. Whether the facilitator is an organizational member or not is generally a matter of preference, but he or she should have the experience and expertise to keep the discussion focused and be highly motivated to help the organization develop a shared vision.

Assessing Where You Are and Have Been

Before beginning to look forward it is important to have a clear sense of the status quo. Understanding where you are starting from is critical to developing a vision that fits with the culture of the organization. In this phase, leaders should identify a plan for vision building and develop a process to assess the activities that the organization currently engages in. Benchmarking during this phase allows organizational members to compare their current processes to those of competitors and provides a framework in which to think about the future goals of the organization.

Contemplating a New Direction

Once a clear understanding is developed of current practices and processes, the organization should begin to think about where it is headed. By this phase, key stakeholders should be identified and their input should be sought to determine how the organization is currently working to meet their needs. An analysis of this input, in light of current practices, should begin to point to areas that might benefit from change.

Building a Vision Together

Once the ideas have begun to emerge for a new direction, the vision must begin to be clearly articulated. The outcome of this phase should be a concise statement of the future direction of the organization. This statement will help organizational members articulate what they do and develop a sense of pride in their work and identification with their organization. This process must include multiple stakeholders, and the final product must be clearly communicated across levels of the organization.

Identifying Roadblocks

After clearly articulating where the organization wants to go and developing a statement that stakeholders can buy into, it is important to recognize where challenges may be encountered. To the extent that potential stumbling blocks can be identified, development of the strategic plan can help to address how those will be dealt with. Taking the time to do this at this stage can help reduce the likelihood of serious setbacks that can be discouraging and demoralizing for organizational members down the road.

Realizing the Organizational Vision

After investing the time and energy into this process, it is important that action be taken immediately to capitalize on the enthusiasm and motivation generated by the process. When a shared vision is created, organizational members may be inspired and optimistic about the new directions that the organization is taking and excited about the role they will play in the process. If implementation of practices designed to move toward fulfillment of the mission is not forthcoming, however, demoralization may set in rapidly.

A clear strategic plan should be developed outlining the goals for vision implementation, and meaningful discussion should be had at all levels of the organization about how such implementation can most effectively be integrated into current systems. As this discussion evolves, the vision for the organization should become more deeply integrated into daily communicative practices in the organization. Job description, performance evaluations, and routine discussions and decision-making practices should reflect the underlying values that are embedded in the organizational vision.

Developing a Self-Monitoring System of Vision Adjustment

We have already addressed the importance of continuously assessing the effectiveness both of the vision and of its implementation. You must, however, establish a clear time frame for assessment at the outset. After a specified time, workshops and performance review sessions should be held to assess the effectiveness of the organizational vision. Identify the questions that are most salient for the particular organizational situation and be prepared to revise those aspects that have not lived up to expectations. Assess realistically how long it should take for new programs to be put in place and be given a chance to be effective. At the review point it should be relatively easy to assess which programs are taking hold more slowly than expected versus those that are not taking hold at all or are producing undesirable results.

Exercise 3.3

- How receptive/resistant to change is the organization that you belong to? What factors influence this cultural attitude? Does this lend strength to your organization or weaken it? How can this help move you toward articulation of a clearer vision?

- Look at this organization and consider the following questions:
  - What is unique about us?
  - What values are true priorities for the next year?
  - What would make me personally commit my mind and heart to this vision over the next several years?
  - What does the world really need that our organization can and should provide?
  - What do I want our organization to accomplish so that I will be committed to, aligned with, and proud of my association with this organization?

▶ Review Questions

▼ What is a long-term vision and why are such visions important?

▼ What are the principal qualities of an effective vision?

▼ What does it mean for a member to identify with the organization? What influences identification?

▼ How would you go about developing an effective vision?

▶ Discussion Questions

▼ Many vision statements seem vague. Even Dilbert makes constant fun of them. What do you believe is "wrong" with most of them or the process by which they are developed?

▼ Think about a vision statement that has been effective. What made it so?

▶ References and Recommended Readings

Allen, R. (1995). On a clear day you can have a vision. *Leadership and Organizational Development Journal, 16*, 39-45.

Cheney, G. (1982). *Organizational identification as process and product.* Unpublished master's thesis, Purdue University.

Lewis, C. P. (1997). *Building a shared vision: A leader's guide to aligning the organization.* Portland, OR: Productivity Press.

Klein, S. (1996). A management communication strategy for change. *Journal of Organizational Change Management, 9*(2), 32-46.

Strebel, P. (1996, May-June). Why do employees resist change? *Harvard Business Review,* pp. 86-92.

Sample Organizational Identification Questionnaire

While filling out the following survey, please think of your daily work routine at your company. For each of the following statements, please circle the response that best describes your belief about, or attitude toward, your company. The possible responses are:

YES!	I agree very strongly with the statement.
YES	I agree strongly with the statement.
yes	I agree with the statement.
?	I neither agree or disagree with the statement.
no	I disagree with the statement.
NO	I disagree strongly with the statement.
NO!	I disagree very strongly with the statement.

1. I am proud to be an employee of my company.
   YES!   YES   yes   ?   no   NO   NO!

2. I'm very concerned about the success of my company and work group.
   YES!   YES   yes   ?   no   NO   NO!

3. When making on-the-job decisions, I consider the consequences of my actions for my company.
   YES!   YES   yes   ?   no   NO   NO!

4. I am bothered when other people criticize my company.
   YES!   YES   yes   ?   no   NO   NO!

5. I like where I think my company is going.
   YES!   YES   yes   ?   no   NO   NO!

6. I would be quite willing to spend the rest of my career with this company.
   YES!   YES   yes   ?   no   NO   NO!

7. The people at my company are different from others in our industry.
   YES!   YES   yes   ?   no   NO   NO!

8. I am willing to put in extra effort in order to help my company be successful.
   YES!   YES   yes   ?   no   NO   NO!

9. My values and my company's values are quite similar.
   YES!   YES   yes   ?   no   NO   NO!

10. I tell my friends that my company is a great organization to work for.
    YES!   YES   yes   ?   no   NO   NO!

11. I usually agree with my company's policies on important matters.
    YES!   YES   yes   ?   no   NO   NO!

12. My job with my company is an important part of who I am.
    YES!   YES   yes   ?   no   NO   NO!

To score, give 7 points for each YES!; 6 for YES; 5 for yes; 4 for ?; 3 for no; 2 for NO; and 1 for NO!. A score about 60 indicates a fairly high degree of identification and employees that are more than willing to contribute to the company's success. Scores from 36-60 indicate that it is just a job and motivation will usually come primarily from work incentives. A score under 36 indicates a major morale/legitimacy problem that is probably contributing to low performance.

SOURCE: Adapted from Cheney (1982).

NOTE: Used with permission.

Guiding Interpretations
and the Art of Framing

People respond to the meanings they have for words and events rather than to the words and events themselves—the statement made is rarely the statement received. This basic communication principle appears obvious but is one of the most frequently overlooked principles in organizational life. The mediation between words and events and the meanings individuals have for them can be well described as a cultural process. The produced meanings in turn circle back to influence what is said and done and the cultural interpretation of these meanings. The management of meaning is the ultimate goal in the choice of specific words and actions.

The most basic process of managing meaning is called *framing.* Framing refers to the ways leaders can use their language to shape or modify particular interpretations of organizational events thereby directing likely responses. Whereas visioning involves the shaping of formal mission statements and espoused values, framing focuses on the everyday communication of organizational metaphors, stories, artifacts, and myths that shape interpretations.

Although these discursive devices are less formally articulated than are their visioning counterparts, they nevertheless play a crucial role in creating and normalizing organizational members' experiences. Like most communication skills, the ability to frame situations in a certain light is a learned process.

This chapter outlines the importance of the interpretive process, shows how language socially constructs interpretive frameworks, and explains how managers can use the process of framing to reinforce and modify an organizational culture and member's experiences and responses.

Key Objectives of the Chapter

▼ To understand the relationship between visioning and framing within the larger cultural model

▼ To understand how language creates, shapes, and reproduces interpretive frames

▼ To gain the ability to use effectively discursive instruments available for framing, including metaphors, stories, traditions, vocabulary, artifacts, contrast, and spin

▼ To identify several framing dangers, including exaggeration, mixed messages, and the way language can marginalize and hide discursive options

▼ To identify and evaluate framing opportunities

Questions to Consider

▼ Have you ever had a discussion where you thought the other person understood you, only to find out later that this person thought something different was meant? Why do you think you had different meanings?

▼ Can you think of a time when two alternative descriptions of an event or decision were possible and one was chosen over the other? What most influenced the choice? How do you see the relation between who said it and what was said?

▼ Have you ever been in a meeting where people's stories seem to have far more weight than the available information? Why are stories sometimes listened to more than data? What makes a story especially effective?

▼ Can you think of a group or organization you are familiar with that uses jargon? If you look carefully at the jargon used, what does it tell you about power relations in the company or the worldview of members?

▼ Try to think of an example where you have heard someone (possibly in the media) attempt to promote a positive "spin" to the understanding of an event. What happened? Why do you think this happened?

▶ The Centrality of Interpretations

The ways we talk about work environments are connected to the way people think about and act in the workplace. As Mawhinney (1998) notes, wording a situation in different terms can elicit different ways of understanding solutions. For example, the statement "Absenteeism causes inefficiency" will most likely elicit questions about how the organization can devise punishments to drive down absenteeism. In contrast, the statement "High attendance is correlated with efficiency" is more likely to evoke discussion about how the organization can devise positive reinforcements to motivate higher attendance. Consider the following dialogue we heard on the street the other day:

Young Man *(after sitting down next to a young woman with an ice cream cone):* "Nice night, isn't it?"

Young Woman: "This isn't a bar!"

Young Man: "Sorry, must be tough being so attractive and having guys hit on you all the time."

Young Woman: "Look, I have a boyfriend."

The dialogue is both rather obvious and straightforward and easily understood by nearly anyone familiar with North American culture. On the other hand, it is quite complex and requires a fair amount of sophistication in hearers for it to be obvious to them. No statement is a direct or a literal response to the one preceding it. In fact, the replies could be interpreted as nonsense, but we did not so interpret them, nor did they. Each statement must be understood or interpreted within some frame of what is being said or done.

Interpretation is deeply cultural. An interaction like this one requires standard social interaction scripts and ways of making statements fit those scripts. And any particular interpretation is always held against competing interpretations worked out in time. One could imagine a number of statements the young man could have made to convince the young woman that this was intended as a casual conversation. And we might never know whether she was deflecting an advance or merely exploring how interested and tenacious he was.

All statements and actions are subject to interpretation and a continued process of struggle over the appropriate frame to be applied.

Even the clearest statement cannot escape this intrinsic quality of human interaction. But careful attention to interpretive processes can aid the management of the process.

When people talk there are always two conversations that can be displayed. The first records the explicit use of words and expressions. The second is the inferred interaction between what people meant and thought the other heard. These are called the "left-hand" and "right-hand" interactions, respectively, because that is how they appear on paper.

Consider the following interaction from a real workplace. Here the so-called right-hand dialogue (the interplay of interpretations) is also displayed:

Says	Means
Joe: "Eric, how long will it take you to do that project?"	*Eric has the information and should participate in this decision.*
Eric: "I don't know? How long should it take?"	*Joe doesn't make any sense. He's the boss. Why doesn't he tell me when to finish it?*
Joe: "You're in the best position to estimate the time requirements."	*Eric won't take responsibility. It's time he learned. I can't work with anybody who does not take responsibility.*
Eric: "Ten days, I guess."	*This is crazy. I don't know. I haven't thought about it, but he's expecting an answer. I'll guess, maybe this is close.*
Joe: "Take fifteen. Sure you can get it done in that time?"	*He'll never get it done in ten days, probably not even fifteen. He doesn't seem to have the ability to estimate time, but we have an agreement.*
Eric: "Okay."	*These are my orders, fifteen days.*

The project actually should have been given about 20 days. So Eric worked overtime and on the weekends. But on the 15th day he still needed another day to finish.

Says	**Means**
Joe: "Are you done and ready to move on?"	*I'll make sure that he fulfills our agreement.*
Eric: "I'll finish it tomorrow."	*I hope he appreciates how hard I have worked to complete his orders.*
Joe: "But we had agreed that it would be ready today."	*I knew he could not get it done. I hope he learns a lesson in responsibility.*
Eric: "I can't work in a place like this."	*What a stupid, incompetent boss! Not only did he give me the wrong orders, but he does not appreciate how hard I worked. I can't work for a person like this.*
Joe: "Huh?"	*Boy, is he temperamental. What's going on here? He must be having problems at home.*

Interactions like this one happen all the time in organizations and usually remain undetected or are written off as the effects of a bad day or a personality problem. Such differences are not the result of ignorance, bad will, incompetence, resistance, or personalities. They are often the result of smart, dedicated people using their competence with the best of intentions. They are using the most basic values and assumptions to make sense. But the basic values and assumptions are different. Similar interactions are especially prone to happen during transitions and cultural change processes, since normal rules of interpretations may no longer be shared and fear and distrust may be higher.

Most people manage the left-hand dialogue with little thought to the right-hand one. Leaders aware of interpretation processes manage the right-hand one with careful selection of words and expressions. Framing is the process of presenting things in such a way as to shape interpretations in a particular way. When framing is successful, meanings are more closely aligned and people are able to see events in new and more interesting and useful ways.

Exercise 4.1

Choose a recent discussion, especially one where you felt misunderstood. Record the left-hand statements as close to literally as you can. Now try to write the implicit right-hand discussion. What meanings were missed? What type of assumptions appear most responsible for the nonalignments?

▶ Why Framing?

> Leaders do not have a choice about whether or not to communicate. They only have a choice about how much to manage what they communicate.
> —*Edwin Schein (1992, p. 253)*

Organizational leaders operate in turbulent environments that are partly of their own making. Although leaders do not and cannot completely control all events, they nevertheless influence how events are seen and understood. Arguably, the most central tool of influence is language. Most leaders spend nearly 70% of their time communicating, but few pay close attention to how their language influences the interpretive frameworks of those around them. Managers who are highly skilled in language can easily produce words and sentences that highlight some values while masking others. Sometimes language is so smooth that it seduces people into believing that many of the so-called facts in our world are objectively, rather than socially, created.

Framing is a quality of communication that leads others to accept one meaning over another. It is a skill with profound effects on how organizational members understand and respond to the world in which they live. It is a skill that most successful leaders possess, yet one that is not often taught. Nevertheless, managers can learn how to manage meaning through framing.

According to Gail Fairhurst and Robert Sarr (1996), framing consists of three key components: language, thought, and forethought. *Language* is the most obvious part of the skill. Through language, managers place focus on aspects of situations that are ambiguous and vague. Language helps to categorize topics in an organized fashion. Through the creation of vibrant stories and metaphors, language helps us to remember information and acts to transform the way in which we view situations. To put language to use, of course, people must first have *thought and reflected* on their own interpretive frameworks and those of others. In the absence of a clear idea of the desired values to be instilled, language cannot work to communicate goals. Last, for framing to be successful, leaders must learn to frame spontaneously in myriad situations. Being able to do so has to do with having the *forethought* to predict framing opportunities. In other words, one must plan in order to be spontaneous.

▶ The Relation of Framing to Visioning and Culture Change

As a part of the change process, leaders can most effectively modify or change organizational culture through the communicative behaviors of visioning and framing. Leaders use vision statements to articulate the organization's goals. Visioning is essential to creating the norms, mission, and rules of an organization, components that make up the organization's formally espoused goals. Thus, we can understand vision to be an organizational *ideal*. Nevertheless, as any experienced manager understands, it is one thing to formulate official goals; it is an entirely different (and possibly more difficult task) to communicate these goals so that they are inculcated in and acted on by employees on a daily basis.

This is where framing comes in. Whereas visioning pertains to the organization's articulated goals, framing involves the everyday behavioral and communicative processes that organizational members use to reach, contradict, or avoid these goals. Leaders frame events through the use of language choices and techniques such as metaphors, artifacts, stories, and myths. Framing helps align everyday understandings with the organization's mission. Leaders can use myriad framing devices to modify interpretive frameworks that are not in concert with the organization's vision.

▶ The Social Construction of Interpretive Frames

When we think of excellent speakers of our time, invariably names like John F. Kennedy, Martin Luther King Jr., and Maya Angelou come to mind. These three speakers have in common a mastery of the English language, a seemingly effortless ability to make pictures from words, and the capacity to mesmerize their audiences with endless streams of rhetorical devices. In addition to being wonderful to listen to, these societal visionaries have literally created a new reality based on their words. When King said in his "I Have a Dream" speech, "America has given the Negro people a bad check—a check which has come back marked 'insufficient funds'" (quoted in Cook, 1985), his words created a reality that needed to be acted on. Through his metaphor, he pointed out the bleak situation that America had created for African Americans. This metaphor, along with many others in the speech, created the urgency needed to set the civil rights movement into action.

Through language, today's managers can also create and fundamentally change people's interpretive frames. When we think of an articulated organizational vision, therefore, it is not so much of a mental conception put into practice as it is a discursive instrument that simultaneously shapes organizational members' behavior and mental activity. Thus, the organization's espoused values are largely self-referential and self-reproducing. Through repeated discourse, the vision becomes an imaginary object and the apparent referent. Thus, the power of language instruments (missions, metaphors, stories, etc.) lies not only in their rhetorical ingenuity but also in their power to constitute and normalize reality.

For instance, let us analyze the concept of *sexual harassment*. For most people today, sexual harassment is conceptualized as a specific object or behavior; namely, it is defined as unwanted and offensive sexual advances or sexually derogatory or discriminatory remarks. Indeed, it is difficult to remember a time when sexual harassment has not existed, but the term itself was first used less than 20 years ago.

Before the term existed, the *object* of sexual harassment as we know it also did not exist. Victims of unwanted sexual advances had only phrases such as "overly friendly" and words such as "uncomfortable" to describe their situation. As one might guess, victims did not have an easy way of explaining their predicament. In the absence of words to describe the situation, most perpetrators were not held accountable for their behavior. Who could be ostracized for merely being "too friendly"? Only since the emergence of the actual phrase, in a late 1970s court case, has the behavior been understood as a concrete legal infraction worthy of punishment.

But establishing a term and various technical definitions does not do away with the contest of meanings, the various ways people struggle over what things mean, in fact what things are. As Robin Clair (1993) has shown, organizational stories about potentially harassing statements and events sometimes dismiss the events as trivial or based in misunderstandings. Other stories shift responsibility to the victim. And still others display hidden sources of power relations questioning what might otherwise be seen as consensual. As Clair showed, these are all cases of framings and the attempt to reach shared interpretations.

As is true in the phrase sexual harassment, sometimes the use of new words or phrases can be helpful for describing a "going-on" that was not previously articulated. Through the normalization of the words, however, it is easy to forget that the concept itself is not a naturally occurring "object." Rather, like all concepts, it is produced through language.

As illustrated in a case study of knowledge-intensive workers (Deetz, 1997), concepts of work ("integrated" and "smokestack") are not simply the naming of different things. The naming creates an important difference, highlights ways things can be seen as unlike and provides more or less favored interpretations. The move of treating these produced objects and their discontinuities and preferences as if they were a property of the world seals the system off from discussion, since it is treated as natural rather than as produced.

Ideas that may seem absolutely normal, real, and unquestionable—for example, business concepts such as productivity, consultancy, and total quality management—are actually produced through language. Close analysis of these concepts by managers can reclaim the constructed quality of these productions, and through framing, leaders can use discursive constructions to produce and change the cultures of their organizations.

▶ ## Discursive Instruments for Framing

Leaders can have a tremendous effect on the interpretive frames of organizational members. What a leader simply pays attention to can have a huge impact on how a program or department functions. If a certain value or program is deemed important, managers can increase its value in organizational members' eyes by consistently asking employees questions about it or including the topic or program on meeting agendas.

Managers should be aware that their emotional blowups send a memorable message to employees. For instance, if an organizational president reacts to a product failure by immediately firing the employees in charge of the product, a message will be sent to others that it is not wise to take risks—a message that the president may not have intended. Behavior speaks louder than words. If leaders want to ensure that their values are inculcated into organizational members, then they must also provide organizational systems that correlate with their espoused goals. One way they can consistently communicate their vision is through framing.

Fairhurst and Sarr (1996) overview many of the important ways to frame situations. In this section, we describe several different discursive framing tools, including metaphors, stories, traditions, jargon and slogans, artifacts, contrast, and spin. Some culture researchers go so far as to conceptualize organizational cultures as *consisting of* these symbols. Although we understand the merits of viewing discursive elements such as stories, metaphors, and myths as constituting a culture, we feel that it is more worthwhile to view these things as *discursive instruments* that actively create, shape, and modify organizational culture. These discursive tools can be viewed as holding a symbolic function, in that they always represent something different or something more than what they are.

Table 4.1 outlines the purpose of each discursive framing tool, offers recommendations about when these tools should be used, and gives a brief example of each.

Metaphor—Comparing One Thing to Another

Metaphors are the most complex and important framing tools for organizational leaders. Like all framing devices, a metaphor is a form of symbolic, rather than literal, expression. *The American Heritage Dictionary of the English Language* (1992) defines a metaphor as, "A figure of speech in which a word or phrase that ordinarily designates one thing is used to designate another, thus making an implicit comparison, as in 'a sea of troubles'" (p. 1134). Metaphors are pleasurable and surprising to listen to because they help us see the ordinary in a new way. In addition to creating vivid word pictures, however, metaphors serve as the essential bridge between the literal and the symbolic, between cognition and

TABLE 4.1 Discursive Framing Tools and Their Use

Discursive Tool	Purpose	Example	Potential Pitfalls
Metaphor	To give an idea or program a new meaning by comparing it to something else.	I think of our office as just one big family. We have our squabbles but that doesn't keep us from working with each other.	They can mask or discourage significant alternative meanings.
Stories (Myths and Legends)	To frame a subject by anecdote in a vivid and memorable way.	In our business, tragedy happens, such as when . . . (story) You can't take it personally.	They can become overused or send mixed messages.
Traditions (Rites, Rituals, Ceremonies)	To pattern and define an organization at regular time increments to confirm and reproduce organizational values.	Annual holiday parties; daily performances such as saying hello to every employee.	They may be nonmeaningful or trite or make it difficult for new meanings to emerge.
Slogans, Jargon, and Catchphrases	To frame a subject in a memorable and familiar fashion.	Calling passengers "punters."	A word or phrase can become loaded, misunderstood, or overused.
Artifacts	To illuminate corporate values through physical vestiges (sometimes in a way language cannot)	Layout of a board room; design of offices/cubicles.	Sometimes they contradict corporate mission.
Contrast	To describe a subject in terms of what it is not.	Our new business plan is nonhierarchical and unobtrusive.	It may do little to define the concept.
Spin	To talk about a concept so as to give it a positive or negative connotation.	"That was a good speaker. She hesitated some, but that just shows she really thought about her answers."	Do not use if the difference between reality and the spin is excessive and unbelievable.

affect, and between the conscious and the unconscious, according to many psychologists. Thus, metaphors are often used to present new ideas and insights in a way not always available within the processes of analytic reasoning and discourse.

Through the use of metaphors, people come to understand and experience one thing (program, concept, idea) in terms of another. Organizations can be metaphorically discussed and thought about in terms of machines, organisms, armies, teams, or families. Each comparison draws attention to certain aspects of organizational life and tends to hide other aspects. The metaphor also can direct decision making and the interpretation of events. An organization that thinks of itself in family terms—produces a family culture—has a very different response to layoff pressures than a culture framed as military or mechanical.

Managers can think of metaphors as figurative analogies that draw comparisons between two dissimilar things. We use these analogies so much in our everyday talk that it is sometimes difficult to identify them. Consider the following examples:

▼ The introduction of a new product is a *baby step* in the right direction.

▼ The impending layoffs are just a *Band-Aid* on the problem.

▼ This office is just one big *family.*

▼ If we don't upgrade our computers soon, the company will *miss the boat.*

▼ The institution of paternal leave *levels the playing field.*

Through figurative analogies, speakers compare unfamiliar situations to those people understand and can identify with.

Likewise, business leaders can use metaphors to explain their corporate vision. Fairhurst and Sarr (1996) discuss how a small group of managers in a public affairs program tried to envision a more productive future for their company. After a concentrated analysis, the managers decided that their mission was threefold: (a) to continue the general information-dissemination activities of any public affairs department, (b) to get buy-in from senior management they needed to responsibly communicate with the public, and (c) to engage in more two-way communication with the public by having employees become members of various stakeholder organizations.

As the public affairs managers surveyed this threefold mission, they realized that their three goals seemed equal and interdependent, yet the overall vision of all three goals was the same: to win public trust. They were struck by the vision's similarity to a three-legged stool. From that point forward, whenever managers discussed their vision, they began with the complex metaphor of the three-legged stool. The metaphor was critical in helping to clarify their thinking and their ability to manage and frame the meaning of their departmental vision.

Stories and Myths

As an organization develops a history, values can be packaged and performed through corporate stories and myths. Myths can be defined as unquestioned, shared beliefs about the benefits of certain routines, techniques, or behaviors that are not supported by demonstrated facts. Stories are often seen as closely linked to the myth (and are often the expression of the myth). Stories, which are often considered to be "gossip," say a lot about how employees believe the organization "really" works. In addition, storytelling performances typify certain experiences as being worthy of emulation or deserving of caution and thus call attention to possible future organizational experiences. The retelling of stories provides insight into the organization's culture and thus its operations. Therefore, stories are a powerful tool for reinforcing organizational assumptions and teaching these assumptions to organizational newcomers.

Managers obviously do not have complete control over the stories passed along in their organizations. Nevertheless, they can strategically use stories to "put a face" on their corporate goals and vision. In addition, stories are memorable and vivid and create rapport. Many times, after people forget organizational rules, regulations, and articulated goals, they nevertheless remember the story or anecdote that illustrated the point. Like all good stories, corporate myths usually include hero and villain characters, a conflict, and a resolution that teaches some type of lesson. Stories can also be humorous, which is often accomplished by making the story familiar to or consistent with the audience's lives.

Consider the following story relayed by a senior 911 operator to another, less experienced operator. As told to us, the story is gruesome, even shocking. It nevertheless illustrates how a story can teach an organizational lesson in a vivid and memorable fashion.

Once a woman called me who found her husband hanging, and was sure he was still alive because when she cut him down, she heard him throw up. [But] that was because when the noose was around his neck [it] had blocked the fluids, so when she took it off, his body was emitting the fluids. Well, she assumed that was a sign he was still alive. You could hear her trying to give him mouth-to-mouth and you could hear him gurgling in the background, and to me, that just completely grossed me out for one, but number two, I felt so bad. . . . Some of the things she was saying, you knew he was dead, but she wasn't, hadn't accepted it. But you have to stay on the line and listen to it whether you want to or not. . . . There are call-takers here that I think go a little too much into personal aspects of the caller or getting too much information. . . . [But] you can't get involved. You just kinda put those things in perspective.

Through the telling of this story, the senior 911 operator does several things. First, she conveys the tragedy inherent to the business. Second, she puts a face on the issue and creates a vivid picture with her words. Last, she conveys the lesson that 911 call takers cannot get too personally involved if they want to survive in the job. In telling a story, the operator made the lesson interesting and memorable to the trainee.

Traditions: Rites, Rituals, Ceremonies, and Celebrations

Based on their collective values and beliefs, organizations also have recurring collective action patterns that symbolically pattern and define organizational life. Rites are collective activities in which employees initiate or conclude a given phase of events. An example of a development rite is when General Motors initiated the Saturn project and hundreds of employees from all different levels met for several days in an off-site area to strategically study the future of the company.

In contrast to the rite, managers use rituals to reproduce and confirm common organizational traditions. The best example is a common meeting. Mike Pacanowsky and Nick O'Donnell-Trujillo (1983) categorize rituals as personal, task, social, or organizational (see Table 4.2). Personal rituals, performed by individuals within the organization, serve as "trademark" performances. They solidify employees' organizational identity as well as inform others about their identity. They are also the critical incidents that employees draw on when they attempt to make sense of particular organizational members and the culture to which they belong. Task rituals can be individual or collective. These types of rituals

TABLE 4.2 Types of Rituals

Type of Ritual	Example of Ritual	Symbolic Implication
Personal	Each and every weekday morning, Jenny, owner of a local real estate office, walks around the office and says, "Good morning" to each employee.	Shows employees that management keeps in touch with and cares about what employees are doing.
Task	At the end of each month, Cathy Clavin, account executive at Stanley Public Relations, meets with her account assistants to go through their date books and time sheets to figure out how much time they collectively spent for each client. Depending on the hours and the work actually produced, Cathy figures out how many hours the client should actually be billed for.	Indicates to subordinates that they should keep detailed records about the time spent servicing clients, but when it comes to billing, there is flexibility beyond solely the hours spent. Quality of work is also important.
Social	Every Thursday night, a group of the ramp servicemen at City Airport go for a beer at one of the airport bars. Talk revolves around sports, women, and union politics.	Upholds a network among the workers outside of work. Identifies membership and status level within a particular organizational subculture.
Organizational	Each summer, the tenured sales people at ABC Marketing invite the new sales recruits to a golf match. Competition is severe and the new recruits have never won.	Represents a status hierarchy between new recruits and tenured employees. Teaches new employees that they should learn from and respect the longer tenured sales people.

continually reveal the day-to-day routines that "get the job done." Social rituals, such as eating lunch outside on the company's patio, are carried out without explicit connection to the organization but nevertheless have the effect of solidifying organizational identification and a sense of belonging to subcultures. Organizational rituals, such as company picnics, board of directors meetings, or executive meetings, are largely analogous to organizational rites. These performances reveal global features of an organization's culture.

Two other more formal events that establish time patterns and traditions in organizations are ceremonies and celebrations. The ceremony is a formal event that usually expresses a sense of organizational tradition and history. Examples of ceremonies include initiations, graduations, anniversaries, the formal launching of a product, and the opening of a new branch. The celebration is a less formal ceremony where more mundane activities take place. An example would be a company's annual holiday party.

Through rites, rituals, ceremonies, and celebrations, organizational leaders can maintain consistency and tradition in the organization that communicates corporate vision and goals.

Slogans, Jargon, and Catchphrases

Every organization has its own special vocabulary that is peculiar to its particular profession or organizational culture. In this vocabulary, we find jargon (words unfamiliar to people outside the culture), slogans, and colloquial catchphrases. They are popular word choices because, like the metaphor, they bring a unique "insider" meaning to the concepts they represent.

As is the case with all discursive instruments, managers cannot always completely control the vocabulary of their employees. In fact, jargon is often specifically used because its meaning is obtuse and indecipherable by outsiders. For example, on a commercial cruise ship, employees referred to passengers not as "guests," as management would have liked, but rather as "punters." Through the use of this term, employees were able to depersonalize their association with the passengers and treat them as faceless consuming robots. We see a similar type of depersonalization occurring when doctors refer to their patients as "ringers" (as in hanging around the ring of the drain, since they are almost "down the drain"), and when 911 call takers refer to callers as "schizoids."

Through framing, however, management can help modify the interpretations of others. In one example, a new beauty salon owner wanted to create a sense of high-class style in her salon. She did so, in part, by requiring all of her employees to speak of their patrons as "clients" rather than as "customers." The word "client" is traditionally associated with important, long-term, business transactions, whereas "customer" brings forth the image of a transitory supermarket patron. Through the use of the word "client," employees were inculcated with the value of building long-term, mutually respectful relationships with the shop's patrons.

A catchphrase or slogan can also do a lot to frame or summarize a group of ideas. One of the most popular conceptions in the 1990s has been "change." Fairhurst and Sarr (1996) discuss how Bill Clinton capitalized on this trend in thinking when his campaign team devised his 1992 campaign slogan, "Don't stop thinking about tomorrow." Through the use of this slogan, Clinton was able to portray a theme of a brighter future. The slogan also created an environment where change could only be thought of as good. The American public was presented with two possibilities: Be a part of progress by voting for Clinton or be a part of stagnation by voting for George Bush. This dualistic choice, of course, was merely an illusion of the slogan. Nevertheless, it was an illusion that helped win Clinton the presidency.

Artifacts

The concept of artifacts is generally used to describe the physical vestiges of an organization, for example, the organization's building, equipment, products, and so on. Artifacts are commonly the most concrete symbolic elements in an organizational culture. The architecture, interior design, and physical layout of a building say a lot about how the organization values creativity, control, and hierarchy.

For instance, the setup of a meeting room often symbolizes the nature of business conducted therein. A round table and comfortable chairs symbolize that the people in the meeting are equals and that the meeting is informal. In contrast, a long thin rectangular table with a "head" chair that is bigger or different than the others indicates a more formal hierarchy and a more serious gathering. Managers are wise to consider how the physicalities of their organization reinforce (or contradict) the goals and vision of their organization.

Contrast

The use of contrast allows managers to describe a program or subject by explaining what it is *not*. In vague situations it may be difficult or impossible to describe what the current situation is. Contrast allows managers to use opposites or alternatives to frame a situation. For instance, the current culture may be indecipherable, conflicted, and confused, so a person may describe it as *lacking* organization, enthusiasm, or vision.

Consider the following hypothetical manager/employee conversation where the manager uses contrast to describe the new participative type of management style the organization is working to develop:

Employee: "I just don't get it. I don't know what I'm supposed to do anymore. No one tells me and then I get frustrated when I do it wrong."

Manager: "Well, that's all part of the new participative management."

Employee: "What's that all about?"

Manager: "Well, we're not going to be telling you exactly what to do anymore. No direct orders, no getting in trouble if you don't do it exactly how we want it. Now you're going to have to use your own initiative."

Employee: "So we're not going to have the weekly goal meetings anymore?"

Manager: "We'll still have meetings, but there won't be a set agenda. Instead it will be more like brainstorming, with everyone involved."

In this example, we see how an ambiguous concept, such as participative management, can be made clearer by contrasting it with something it is *not*.

Spin

Spin, defined as the ability to portray a certain person, program, or idea in a positive or negative light, is probably the riskiest of framing tools. Managers can responsibly use positive spin to frame a program (such as their vision) in terms of its strengths, and negative spin to frame other programs (such as competing subcultures) in terms of their weaknesses. Nevertheless, spinning can create a negative response when the amount of spin begins to depart substantially from the reality of the situation at hand. In other words, when the difference between spin and reality becomes large, credibility is lost.

Usually, when we hear the word spin, images of velvet-tongued publicity people come to mind. Indeed, we speak of people who are especially good at the art in a derogatory manner, calling them "spin doctors." Washington of late is filled with them. Journalists who covered the Lloyd Bentsen-Dan Quayle debate spoke of the excessive amount of spin taking place. As the CBS reporter Leslie Stahl said, "We reporters were more than just spun tonight, we were twirled, we were twisted, we were

Cuisinarted" (Brydon, 1989, as cited in Fairhurst & Sarr, 1996, p. 115). Although spin can be used in a responsible and helpful manner, it can easily become a detriment when it crosses the line to blatant exaggeration.

Exercise 4.2

● What discursive instruments (e.g., stories, myths, metaphors, etc.) do you currently see working in organizations or groups in your life? Are the framing tools consistent with articulated goals? Do these discursive instruments make it difficult for alternative conceptions to emerge?

● How can discursive instruments promote one line of thought over another? Provide an example, real or hypothetical, to illustrate your answer. How, if at all, could this benefit the interests of one organizational coalition over another?

▶ The Dangers of Framing

We have already briefly discussed how managers do not always have direct control over how discursive tools are used. We have also explained how managers can lose credibility if they exaggerate a positive or negative spin to the point of not being in touch with reality. In this section we discuss two other dangers of framing.

That Which Highlights Also Marginalizes

In this chapter we have focused on how managers can use different discursive tools to manage the way others see the world. As discussed, language can fundamentally create or modify the way people view reality. This can be a good thing in business when leaders use language to create a reality that keeps their business competitive and is fair to employees. Nevertheless, as much as language can highlight one way of viewing the world, it simultaneously makes it harder to see other, possibly more valid, ways of viewing it.

For instance, if we take another look at Bill Clinton's 1992 campaign slogan, "Don't stop thinking about tomorrow," it obviously highlights the importance of the future. Nevertheless, as Fairhurst and Sarr (1996) note, it also pushes aside the importance of learning from our past. It may also have also discouraged voters to investigate Clinton's personal past. Likewise, although the aforementioned metaphor of the three-legged stool does a good job representing interdependent support, it does little to speak of innovation or the need to take care of oneself.

As discussed, myths and stories serve as core beliefs that are rarely questioned or tested, and as such, they function as a powerful, sometimes insidious type of control. For instance, a popular myth in Western organizations is that people can "pull themselves up by the bootstraps" and can make it "to the top" if they just try hard enough. Yet the data do not support the fact that everyone has the same statistical opportunity for organizational success. Because the bootstrap myth is so pervasive in Western society, however, people take it for granted that any person—despite that person's race, class, or gender—can succeed if he or she only tries hard enough. According to the myth, if a person does not succeed, he or she just did not try hard enough. This type of silent assumption can lead to continued discriminatory structures in the workplace. Myths and stories, although powerful framing tools, can serve to obscure important realities in organizations when they are unquestioned or unexamined.

In Deetz's (1997) case study of knowledge-intensive workers, we also see several framing dangers as well as benefits. The descriptors of "consultancy" versus "funded" and integrated" versus "smokestack" services were normalized in the workplace studied. Through their repeated unquestioned use, the contrasts became taken for granted and obscured discussion options. Admittedly, the concepts of consultancy and integrated solutions had clear values and considerable rhetorical power. Nevertheless, as with all language, the terms were partial in what they highlighted, what they covered up, what they misrecognized, and how they seemed neutral yet favored particular interests and groups of people.

Framing instruments are important tools for communicating organizational vision, but they can also close off certain discursive options. In choosing framing tools, managers should analyze how their language both accents and marginalizes different ideas, values, and groups of people.

Avoiding Mixed Messages

Although organizational leaders have the time to work and rework formal organizational visions until they sound exactly right, the same advantage is not available for the practice of framing. Because framing is often a spontaneous process, managers must be extra careful to avoid sending mixed messages. Managers must ask themselves whether the metaphors, stories, vocabulary, rituals, and artifacts they use in the organization are consistent with each other.

For example, if participative management is the vision, the leader may want to replace closed-door offices with open-air cubicles, rethink the ritual of top management eating out at restaurants while middle managers eat at their desk, replace the use of competitive sports and war metaphors with those that refer to family and teamwork, or quit labeling a certain group of people in a way that shuts them off from high-level strategic planning decisions (such as calling computer people "techies").

If different framing tools contradict each other, employees can become confused and disillusioned about the organizational vision. Of course, it may not be possible for managers to plan out every framing opportunity so it is perfectly in line with vision. An important first step, however, is just being cognizant of all the framing opportunities available and analyzing how those opportunities are used, abused, or ignored.

▶ Recognizing Framing Opportunities

Through the creation of a vision, organizational leaders can map out for themselves the goals and values of their organizational ideal. A vision, however, is only truly effective when it is communicated to others, and this is done through framing. When do opportunities for framing present themselves? Gaps in understanding from employees can be used by leaders to instill or reinforce company vision. Unfortunately, many managers view these gaps as problems rather than framing opportunities. The most natural time to clarify organizational goals, however, is when employees are confused and seeking direction from management.

Using Knowledge Gaps as Framing Opportunities

For employees to identify with a company's vision and culture, they must not only understand new ideas, but they must also see how new programs and ideas relate to the job. It is important that employees understand how new programs fit with old structures. Corporate leaders can encourage enthusiasm and buy-in to new programs by asking employees to devise future steps in implementing goals. Together, these tasks can be accomplished in large part through management communication and framing.

For instance, through vibrant stories and metaphors, leaders can spread enthusiasm about a new program; when employees display confusion about how new goals affect their department, leaders can take this time to reinforce the company vision and explain directly how the employees are an integral part of it; when employees ask about future organizational systems, leaders can frame these projects in terms of future vision.

Understanding the Interpretive Frames of Others

To help others expand their interpretive frames to encompass organizationally espoused values, managers should take the time to understand and be sensitive to others' interpretive frames. In other words, like any persuasive speaker, leaders must know their audience. By taking the time to understand others' interpretive frameworks, employees' knowledge gaps can be seen as opportunities and the occasions for framing become endless—whether they occur during formal meetings, in the elevator, or at the company softball game.

Planning to Be Spontaneous

One of the most common dilemmas about framing is that it cannot be completely planned out. Nevertheless, with some practice and forethought, managers can get into the habit of framing. Managers should envision future situations that are likely to recur in their organization. They can do this by using past incidents, meetings, and conversations as models of probable future ones. Through paying attention to recurring communicative situations, managers can see where linkages can be made between everyday conversations and the organizational vision. The following questions, suggested by Schein (1992) and Fairhurst and

Sarr (1996, p. 164), can be used as a guide by leaders to plan for "spontaneous" framing opportunities:

1. What types of situations continually recur in my organization?

2. Where do employees get their information, and how can I shape this information source?

3. In what areas are employees confused or misinformed, and how can I clarify issues?

4. When and why do employees complain, and what do they complain about?

5. When do employees tell exaggerated stories or offer fallacious reasoning? How can I counter this?

6. How can I provide critical socialization opportunities for new employees?

7. What types of rituals and organizational crises punctuate the organization? How can I frame them in a way that promotes organizational vision?

After asking themselves these questions and analyzing their framing opportunities, managers should trust their gut instinct on framing opportunities. As with any new behavior, when people first prepare for framing opportunities, they may seem awkward and anything but spontaneous. This force of habit, in turn, makes it possible for managers to respond as if they had time to prepare. The only way to become skillful at framing is through trial and error and the continual communication with each other to figure out new ways of understanding organizational concepts or programs. Through continuous planning and communication, framing will become more natural and spontaneous.

This chapter has detailed the many different ways language can create and modify interpretive frameworks and how framing is the integral counterpart to organizational visioning. We have explained the different discursive tools managers can use to frame situations so they are consistent with corporate goals and warned of several dangers of framing. Now the question is, where do we go from here? Although every leader finds his or her own way of going about the art of framing, the following exercise provides some general tips for getting started.

Exercise 4.3

• What framing opportunities present themselves on a regular basis in an organization or group you're involved in? Do you believe the leaders in these organizations make use of framing opportunities?

• Choose a recent situation in a company or group you are involved in where meaning was contested. You might choose a particular problem and pair it with a goal or organizational ideal (e.g., maybe an organization is having a problem with regular attendance and the ideal is that at least 90% of members attend each meeting).

   - List key elements that are necessary for others to understand the present problem and the desired ideal. Create word images you could use to describe the events to ensure clarity, consistency, and comprehension.

   - Formulate a parallel list of discursive framing tools that correlate with the descriptions for the "ideal."

   - As part of this list, attempt to devise a complex metaphor that will illustrate the ideal you are reaching for. Brainstorm on ways that other discursive tools, such as stories, slogans, rituals, spin, and contrast, can be incorporated in the metaphor.

▶ Review Questions

▼ Why is the process of interpretation so critical to communication?

▼ Why is framing an important leadership tool?

▼ How does framing relate to visioning and to the larger cultural concept?

▼ How does language help to "socially construct" people's ways of thinking about events?

▼ What is the value of considering framing tools (e.g., metaphors, stories) as "instruments" rather than as components that "constitute" culture?

▼ What are the advantages and disadvantages of different framing tools?

▶ Discussion Questions

▼ Given that people often interpret words and events differently, what are the possible costs of not taking into account the interpretive frames of others?

▼ If the message sent is often not the message received, who is most responsible for aligning meanings, the sender or receiver? Explain.

▼ How are the meanings of events and decisions shaped in your organization? What do you see as the benefits and costs of this way of doing it?

▼ Think of a time when the meaning of an event or decision was not managed well in an organization or group you belong to. What were the consequences? How could the meaning have been managed differently?

▶ References and Recommended Readings

American Heritage Dictionary of the English Language. (1992). (3rd ed.). Boston: Houghton Mifflin.

Clair, R. (1993). The use of framing devices to sequester organizational narratives: Hegemony and harassment. *Communication Monographs, 60,* 113-136.

Cook, S. (Director). (1985). *Great speeches* (Vol. 1) [videorecording]. Greenwood, IN: Educational Video Group.

Deetz, S. (1997). The business concept and managerial control in knowledge-intensive work: A case of discursive power. *Case studies in organizational communication: 2* (pp. 173-202). New York: Guilford Press.

Fairhurst, G., & Sarr, R. (1996). *The art of framing.* San Francisco: Jossey-Bass.

Mawhinney, T. C. (1998). Editorial. *Journal of Organizational Behavior Management, 18,* 1-6.

Pacanowsky, M., & O'Donnell-Trujillo, N. (1983). Organizational communication as cultural performance. *Communication Monographs, 50,* 127-147.

Palmer, I., & Dunford, R. (1996). Reframing and organizational action. *Journal of Organizational Change Management, 9,* 12-25.

Schein, E. (1992). *Organizational culture and leadership* (2nd ed.). San Francisco: Jossey-Bass.

▶ Suggested Case Study

Deetz, S. (1997). The business concept and managerial control in knowledge-intensive work: A case of discursive power. In B. D. Sypher (ed.), *Case studies in organizational communication* (Vol. 2, pp. 173-202). New York: Guilford Press.

5

Employee Participation and Cultural Change

Up to this point much of the discussion has focused on the direct activities of the leader in building a business and changing or shaping a culture. But increasingly, business leaders have come to understand the value of widespread employee participation in decision making and in change processes. Commanding visions are often best achieved through discussion processes involving organization members from several places and levels in the organization.

Furthermore, the most common changes taking place in organizations today include increased employee participation. The move to most versions of TQM and teams requires a culture of participation where management functions differently and decisions and responsibility are diffused in the organization. Wider participation in creating a culture of participation may seem an obvious need but is often not the case. Management direction alone of cultural change or of participation and empowerment rarely succeeds.

This chapter discusses the reasons for the move to greater employee participation, introduces management philosophy changes necessary in a move to increased employee decision making, considers the situations where participation appears most important, introduces core issues in empowerment from a cultural perspective, provides methods of joint visioning and change, and discusses communication skills necessary for effective participation.

Key Objectives of the Chapter

▼ To understand the forces pushing organizations to wider participation by members and external stakeholders

▼ To recognize the differences in management philosophies when governed by hierarchical control or when governed by participation

▼ To identify situations where participation is of value and who should be involved

▼ To understand the nature of empowerment

▼ To be able to foster greater initiative from others

▼ To be able to use various form of participation in cultural change efforts

▼ To develop basic interpersonal and collaborative skills to enhance organizational dialogue

Questions to Consider

▼ When have you felt that your ideas really mattered to an organization of which you are a part? What did others do to let you know that? How did it change how you felt and acted during your involvement?

▼ Under what circumstances do you feel organizational members take initiative? What hampers the taking of initiative?

▼ Who do you feel is most invested in the well-being of an organization with which you are familiar? Why are they invested in this way?

▼ What do you think of empowerment? When has it been real? What were the consequences?

▼ Do you feel most meetings in organizations are productive? Why or why not?

▼ Do you feel most meetings are primarily directed toward discussion where people express or advocate their point of view or inquiry where people attempt to acquire a greater understanding?

▶ **Employee Participation and Cultural Change**

Greater employee participation in all aspects of running organizations seems to be ensured in the future. No single quality of management practice is more highly correlated with success. When done well, no single management change has more consistently led to improved performance. Nonetheless, motives for the move to greater employee participation are often mixed and implementations have not been uniformly successful.

Successful initiation of a culture of participation and participation in cultural change requires some understanding of (a) the forces leading to participation, (b) challenges to dominant values and assumptions, and (c) the characteristics of situations where participation is especially important.

Forces Leading to Greater Employee Participation

Many of the forces leading to advantages for greater employee participation are similar to those leading to managing culture. Markets are more turbulent. Creativity and innovation are more important. Traditional surveillance and control are more difficult and costly. Additionally, the following are of special interest:

Globalization. Companies often design, manufacture, and sell in several different countries. In such a context, the need for both independence and interdependence increase while the time available to coordinate activities decreases. Hierarchical structures are too slow and cumbersome to meet the situationally specific needs for a decision.

Information Availability. In traditional workplaces managers were often primarily collectors, sorters, and diffusers of information. Much of their time was spent providing interpretations of data. Information technologies allow instant sharing of relevant information, making possible more context-specific interpretations. With available information, employees can better manage their own activities if guided by shared cultural interpretative processes.

Worker and Work Process Changes. The presence of a highly skilled workforce usually means that employees are more desirous and capable of making good decisions. Today, individual qualities account for a greater part of the value added in a work stream. As technologies replace manual labor, time and talent can be better used for decision making.

Consumer Demand and Customization. As the consumer has acquired a greater variety of offerings and greater ability to shop around, the need for quick, customized responses to customers is greater. Often only the frontline person has the capacity to provide that. Such an employee must be empowered to be able to respond.

Employee Commitment and Loyalty. As shown earlier, the new social contract at work has produced an employee who has to look out for his or her own interests. At the same time the value of key employees and the costs of self-serving behaviors have become greater. Nothing increases commitment and loyalty like participation in decision making. To be listened to and to have a stake in the outcomes are powerful forces.

Payoffs. No force has been more powerful in the move to employee participation than the payoffs companies have received. Product quality, productivity, reduced absenteeism, and satisfaction have consistently correlated with high levels of participation. In many cases, employees simply make better decisions than managers. They are often closer to the factors influencing success, they represent greater decisional diversity, and they are often more willing to put the health of the company ahead of personal interests.

Changes in the Conception of Governance

Despite the payoffs and pressures for higher levels of employee participation, business leaders have not been uniform in the degree or manner in which than have embraced it. Many have implemented programs of greater involvement hoping for greater loyalty and commitment without seeking genuine input. Such an approach finally breeds cynicism and diminishes the value of employee insights.

Patricia McLagan and Christo Nel (1995) have shown convincingly that if participation is to truly pay off it cannot be partial. The successful move from bureaucracy and authoritarianism to participation requires

TABLE 5.1 Differences in Hierarchical Control and Participation

Hierarchical Control	Participation
Managers think, employees do.	People in various roles think about the same things from different perspectives.
People in senior positions manage.	People self-manage wherever possible. Senior managers coach and facilitate.
People at the top matter most. Many systems serve them and their information needs.	Everyone's rights, accountability, and dignity are supported and honored.
Knowledge is an important asset for personal power. Teaching moves downward.	Learning and sharing knowledge are key values. People teach each other in all directions.
Shareholders are primary or exclusive stakeholders	Customers, shareholders, employees, and future generations are stakeholders.

SOURCE: Based on McLagan and Nel (1995, p. 25).

a deep change in concepts of governance and assumption regarding the management process. These impact on nearly every activity in the workplace. Table 5.1 captures the fundamental differences.

Exercise 5.1

* Describe places in an organization you know where member participation has increased. What do you feel were the dominant motives for increased participation? How did underlying values and motives influence how participation was practiced and received by members? Were important benefits received by the organization? What type of benefits?

* Describe the places where hierarchical control and participation exist in your organization. Does one dominate? What are the underlying values or assumptions about people and the world that keep each in place?

Times and Places Where Participation Really Pays Off

Although participation clearly has general payoffs, the payoff is optimized under certain situations.

Need for Diverse Insights and Forms of Knowledge. Member participation is especially important when successful choices require diverse insights and forms of knowledge. Such insights and knowledge forms are often acquired experientially and are hard for the management to know or understand fully. Cross-functional teams have been very successful in these contexts. Cultural change efforts nearly always require such diversity. Specific understandings that exist in different parts of the company can only be well represented by those there.

Need for Innovation and Creativity. Innovation and creativity are highly dependent on diversity. As much as leaders encourage others to think outside the box, they and those close to them are not often the best at it. Their ways of thinking and shared sources of information often produce a type of groupthink in even the best intentioned. Thinking out of the box requires others who really think differently. Diverse individuals may each have his or her box, but synergy often arises as different boxes collide. Not all organizational problems require innovative, creative thinking, but those that do require participation.

Need for High Levels of Commitment. During the development of new products, transitions and crises, and cultural change, high levels of commitment are needed. When organizational members participate, they are able to take ownership of the processes and activities that help them play a role in fulfilling the vision. Most members have a need to get more out of work than a paycheck. We all want to feel that we are accomplishing something important, that we are making a difference. When members of an organization feel a commitment to the goals of the organization, they feel as though by helping the organization succeed, they are able to not only be a part of a successful enterprise but also help accomplish something important.

Exercise 5.2

Describe some decisions in your organization that would have benefited from greater participation. Who would you have involved? How would you have ensured adequate diversity of perspectives?

Who Should Participate?

Most of the discussion in this book has focused and will continue to focus on selecting employees who should engage in change processes. Identification with the mission and goals of the organization is increased when the vision is co-created with organizational members. Different members of the organization have key insights and contacts that aid vision formation and change. But individuals who are not formally organizational members also have a stake in the organization's direction. Including them in development of and identification with the vision increases the support the organization receives from a broader constituency and the broadened knowledge base from which decisions are made.

Beyond those who have an economic stake in the success of an organization, there are many others who benefit from or are harmed by the organization's activities. The products produced or services provided affect a wide range of people. Identifying who is affected by the daily operations of the organization helps identify other individuals whose perspectives should help shape the organization's development. One can ask, how do production processes affect those that live in the communities where the organization's sites are located? To whom are services provided? What effect does the organization have on local environments? How do development plans stand to impact different populations?

Exercise 5.3

Think of an organization with which you are associated and consider the following questions. By answering these questions you can begin to assess who might have a vested interest in helping to shape the direction of your organization. Once you have done this, the challenge becomes the development of a realistic plan for including them in the visioning process without irreparably sacrificing the efficiency of the process.

- Who has an economic stake in the success of your organization?
- How is the local community affected by your operations?

- What is the scope of the company's impact (local, national, global)?
- Who is affected by the humanistic activities engaged in?
- What is the environmental impact of organizational activities?
- Who may benefit or suffer from that impact?
- How do company policies impact the families of employees?

Identifying key stakeholders is important for several reasons. On the practical front, stakeholders such as stockholders, local communities, and contracting partners have an economic interest in the success of the organization. These stakeholders want to know that the vision that the organization has for the future is worthy of a financial investment and is likely to bring them dividends of some sort. The more identified they are with the vision of the organization, the more stable a resource they will be. Some stocks are bought and traded daily based on market trends with the sole intent of making profits. Some stocks, however, are held over the long term because the stockholders have an enduring faith in the vision of the organization. They are willing to weather those times that are not as strong or lucrative because they have faith that the long-term vision is one that will bring rewards in the long run.

Today, more and more public policy decisions are being made at the corporate and organizational levels. When these decisions bear on community life, economic systems, and environmental health, those who stand to be affected by the outcomes must be involved in the decision-making processes. Although it is generally unrealistic to expect to include all such stakeholders in every decision that is made without sacrificing great degrees of efficiency, initial involvement in the development of the vision can provide valuable insight into the wants, needs, and concerns of a broad stakeholder constituency. When stakeholders help to shape the direction of the organization and that organization is true to its commitment to use its vision as a framework for effective decision making, awareness of a range of perspectives is brought to bear on each decision made.

This can, in turn, further enhance the commitment of organizational members. Although employees have a financial stake in the success of the organization and want to feel that the work that they are doing is meaningful and important, they generally have a broader stake in the organization as well. Members typically live in the communities in which the organization is located, and their lives and those of their families are affected by organizational decisions. Members who feel that they are working for an organization that is helping to contribute to the growth, stability, and health of the community in which they live are more likely to take pride in the work that they do. This can also enhance feelings of pride in and commitment to the organization in which they are employed.

When key stakeholders are considered and consulted in the process of developing a vision for the organization, it is reflected in the culture of the workplace and manifest in the commitment of members. When vision is lacking or the vision is not shared, the organization may often struggle with lack of focus, frequent turnover, or quality assurance problems. (See Table 5.2.)

▶ Questions Regarding Empowerment

Few doubt that the time of command and control hierarchies is past. Members are being asked and allowed to take initiative, be creative, and accept direct responsibility for their decisions. Discussion of these changes often goes under the broad term *empowerment*. What empowerment means, however, is anything but consistent across organizations or people in organizations. Implementation has often been difficult and met with resistance at all levels. Many of the problems and lack of payoff arise from the different concepts of and motives for empowerment.

The presence of a strong culture aids the move to empowerment. Widely shared values and assumptions aid coordination of independent decision making and help upper managers trust other employees to fulfill organizational objectives. But a strong culture, especially if conformity is expected as a cultural feature, can undermine the innovative and diversity values of empowerment, hence reducing organizational adaptation and learning. Empowerment can aid cultural change and the move to a more innovative strong culture. How all this works out is largely based on answers to central questions. Robert Quinn and Gretchen Spreitzer (1997) develop the following questions of concern:

TABLE 5.2 Employee Participation In Workplace Decisions

What Are the Payoffs?

Higher quality decisions (the biggest benefit), especially in situations where creativity and innovation are critical.

A reduced need for directly supervising and monitoring work behavior.

Reduced turnover due to the increased commitment of employees.

Increased product quality and customization of products for customers.

A greater sense of well-being among employees, who usually take better skills and attitudes home to their communities and families.

An emergence of working arrangements more sensitive to the needs of women and culturally diverse groups.

An increase in the total organizational learning and skills of employees and management.

Signs of Partial or Incomplete Participation

There's no connection between participation activities and reward structures.

Management talks a lot about empowering people as if this is something that can or needs to be done to people.

To justify participation activities, managers stress the need for buying into the corporate ideology or increasing employees' loyalty or commitment. Increasing the quality of decisions is not used as a justification.

Workers only participate in decision making regarding minor issues or those involving the plan for executing higher-up decisions.

Participation groups lack diversity or are "safe."

The company uses participation forums primarily for letting off steam rather than decision making.

Decisions—but not responsibility—are assigned downward.

Key information for decision making is not shared.

Participation programs are suspended during change and crisis.

Before Committing to Participation

Make sure you really want it!

Commit to the long-term. It may well take 18 months or so to see a payoff.

Make sure everyone gets appropriate training. Every person in the company has to overcome years in authoritarian-style training. Training displays management's commitment to a participatory workplace.

Participation skills are not natural; they are acquired over time.

Have your program regularly assessed by outsiders.

What Do You Mean by Empowerment?

Leading executives clearly differ on what they mean by empowerment. Quinn and Spreitzer (1997) found two distinctly different positions in their interviews with executives. They are characterized in the five contrasts shown in Table 5.3 for mechanistic and organic models.

TABLE 5.3 Mechanistic and Organic Approaches to Empowerment

Mechanistic	Organic
Start at the top	Start at the bottom with employee needs
Clarify the organization's mission, vision, and values	Model empowered behavior
Clearly specify the tasks, roles, and rewards	Build teams to encourage cooperation
Delegate responsibility	Encourage intelligent risk taking
Hold people accountable for results	Trust people to perform

SOURCE: Based on Quinn and Spreitzer (1997, p. 38).

Both approaches to empowerment have their time and place, but the organic approach is more likely to create a culture of innovation and deep commitment. Cultural change processes practiced organically are less predictable but are more likely to create conditions where members have integrated their own values with larger values shared by the organization. And such cultures are more able to withstand latent resistance. Much of the popular literature on empowerment works from the mechanistic model. This popularity is based more on catering to managerial fears and identities than careful reasoning or data.

The combination of a communicative leadership articulating a powerful vision and an organic empowerment process enable both leadership and members to make the vision their own. Open discussion rather than the expectation of compliance is key to successful change and empowerment. Many managers have difficulty making a distinction between *leading* the organization and *controlling* it. Empowerment requires such a distinction.

> One group feared empowerment would create "loose cannons." A person from the second group retorted, "When was the last time you saw a cannon of any kind around here."
>
> —*Quinn and Spreitzer (1997, p. 39)*

What Is an Empowered Person?

The popular management literature argues for empowerment based on information sharing, a participatory structure, team building and team-based decision making, relevant training opportunities, and rewarding employees for risk and initiatives. All of these are clearly part of developing an empowered employee, but they retain a concept that empowerment is something that managers do to employees.

In contrast, as Alan Frohman (1997) showed in his studies of personal initiative, meaningful empowerment arises from self-determination and internal motivation. These are likely to be reduced by the values implicit in typical empowerment programs. The assumptions made about people embedded in most empowerment programs have more consequences than the activities. Empowerment requires that leaders help build a culture of initiation and remove barriers. Recognizing initiators helps.

Frohman (1997) argues that in most companies the people who bring about changes are relatively easily recognized, if somewhat unexpected. Most initiators are not on the company's "high potential" list, a list that often represents game playing and conformity. Instead, they are people who perceive organizational needs and take it on themselves to go beyond their jobs. They are action oriented and sufficiently motivated to make a difference so that they often engage in learning focused on meeting organizational needs. Initiators were energetic and independent and openly questioned the status quo but were loyal and respectful.

Do You Need Empowered People?

The reasons for empowerment in a general sense are clear in the reason for moving to participation at all. If employees are desired who are more effective, innovative, and transformational, empowerment is important. Empowered employees do their jobs better, they create new ways of working, they help the organization adapt to changing environments, and they ignite change in those around them. Despite this, many leaders are themselves resistant to empowerment.

Do You Want Empowered People?

Despite the rhetoric not all leaders who advocate empowerment want it. Some are like parents who want their children to make decisions for themselves but want them to make only the decisions that the parent otherwise would have made. Such an approach is often worse than no empowerment at all. It invites mutual distrust and cynicism and cannot achieve the value of employee-based decision making and responsibility. The end result is a workforce of people who ask just to be told what to do and managers who have their beliefs confirmed that employees cannot, will not, or do not want to do it.

Part of the reason for this situation is that bureaucratic cultures are very powerful in many organizations. They are based in deeply held values and assumptions and perpetuated in virtually all talk and practices in organizational life. The thinking and information leading to a desired change is undermined by the larger culture. Expectations of conformity and narrowly defined and highly constrained conflict are common. Lowering these barriers to change is difficult and has to be based in a genuine desire for change. A cultural change process that does not practice the very values desired in the end is not likely to succeed.

How Do People Develop a
Sense of Empowerment?

People develop a sense of empowerment and internalize new values incrementally over time. Doing so demands a willingness to embrace uncertainty and trust people. Trust requires trying and testing.

Change is initiated with reframings that allow individuals to visualize themselves and their environments differently. This begins to show up in new interpretations of situations and new solutions to old problems. Initially, this may be done tentatively and with much attention to others' reactions. Habits are being broken, but even with success, experience has taught many employees to be cautious.

If these actions are reinforced, self-confidence increases and the new patterns become more automatic and comfortable. Commitment to the organization increases as does trust of others, which in turn leads to satisfaction and higher levels of effort. And the cycle continues. Frustration or perceived punishment early in this cycle stops the process quickly and leads to demoralization, leaving the employee more cautious than before.

What Organizational Characteristics
Facilitate Empowerment?

Many qualities of organizational life can facilitate the development cycle. The most central quality is a powerful vision based in the member's own understanding of the challenges facing the organization, one that provides critical internal motivation. Equally important are a group of practices that identify and reward reframing and initiative. Teamwork can provide a circle of people who support each other's efforts. Identifying and expressing stories of accomplishment helps. Tying reward systems to initiative makes the message clear.

The right kind of guidelines can also help. If employees know clearly the situations in which they have discretionary control and where they do not, uncertainty and insecurity are reduced and managers may be more willing to let go of control.

What Can Leaders Do?

Leaders can do much to create organizational conditions that encourage and reduce barriers to initiation and a sense of empowerment. Initiation is often stifled by time pressures, time to get approvals, number of approvals required, inadequate resources, shifting priorities, and complex organizational structures. Leaders have some control over each of these.

But as the work of Quinn and Spreitzer (1997) demonstrated, most importantly leaders must feel empowered themselves; unempowered people rarely empower others. They suggest a list of eight questions for every leader. These "hard and harder" questions serve as an important point of reflection at this point in the chapter.

Exercise 5.4

Think of an organization in which you are a member or imagine yourself as a member of one with which you are familiar. Carefully think through Quinn and Spreitzer's (1997) hard and harder questions.

Hard Questions for a Leader

1. If a sense of a clear strategic vision is a characteristic of an empowering environment, am I continuously working to clarify the sense of strategic direction for the people in my own stewardship?

2. If openness and teamwork are characteristics of an empowering environment, am I continuously striving for participation and involvement for the people in my own stewardship?

3. If discipline and control are characteristics of an empowering environment, am I continuously working to clarify expectations regarding the goals, tasks, and lines of authority in my own stewardship?

4. If support and security are characteristics of an empowering environment, am I continuously working to resolve the conflicts among the people in my own stewardship?

Harder Questions

1. To what extent do I have a sense of meaning and task alignment, and what can I do to increase it?

2. To what extent do I have a sense of impact, influence, and power, and what can I do to increase it?

3. To what extent do I have a sense of competence and confidence to execute my work, and what can I do to increase it?

4. To what extent do I have a sense of self-determination and choice, and what can I do to increase it? (p. 47)

▶ Methods of Participation in Change

In most cases, methods of participation in change efforts differ little from methods for participation in general. Most of these are familiar and need not be repeated here. A great deal of the literature focuses on building effective teams. Deborah Harrington-Mackin's (1994) work is recommended as especially helpful. Other methods more directly connected to joint visioning and developing cultural change are less familiar. Here two will be considered: *appreciative inquiry* and *future and search conferencing*.

Appreciative Inquiry

David Cooperrider and Suresh Srivasta (1990) have developed appreciative inquiry as a way to look at what gives life to an organization. It uses a form of positive questioning to develop a database out of which members can envision more provocative and positive futures. The process is developed out of questions related to discovery, destiny, dream, and design:

Discovery: What is it about the organization that should be appreciated and valued? What gives life to the organization? What in the organization is exceptional?

Destiny: What can be learned in the process of inquiry that can lead to sustainable change and growth? Who would be involved? Who shares in the organization's destiny?

Dream: What are the possibilities for the organization's future? What would we like? What would we like to be doing?

Design: How would an organization look that meets that future? How can we remake the organization to prepare for reaching our dream?

In such an approach, data gathering, development of future possibilities, and building commitment to those possibilities are combined. As a group participates in the inquiry process, the ordinary problem-solving mode of thinking that often stymies change and strips groups of their energy is redirected toward making futures rather than getting by. Groups that focus their energy on their preferred futures exhibit more energy and commitment than groups that discuss their past and present problems. Systematic questioning can provide reframing that is difficult to advocate or would otherwise be met with resistance.

Future and Search Conferencing

Future and search conferences are based on a similar logic but use the focus and energy generated in retreat settings for an organization to move from exploration to commitment more quickly. Future and search conference methodologies have been around for some time but recently have been heralded as new social innovations in the field of managing large-scale change.

Conferences of this sort use the energy involved in intense systematic discussion to help organizations find a course to the future and adapt to turbulent environments. They are normally two-to three-day events away from the work site. Participants are selected based on knowledge and insight, diversity of perspective, ability to engage in open communication, and potential for taking responsibility for implementation. More details are provided in the review by Ronald Purser and colleagues (Purser & Cabana, 1997) of such a conference with Xerox.

▶ Developing Principles of Dialogue

Participation that makes a difference is based in a very different form of communication than that common in command and control management and debating societies. This form is best described as dialogue. Peter Senge (1990) described dialogue as the capacity of a group to suspend assumptions and enter into a genuine "thinking together." He does not mean "thinking alike," for which one person would do, but a type of interaction where prior stances are let go and individuals engage in productive explorations and conflicts that push beyond the thinking of any one person.

This is clearly different from talk in most organizations that emphasize advocating particular choices without exploring underlying intents and assumptions and usually do not pursue win/win decisions. Dialogue requires both particular qualities of interpersonal communication and a collaborative orientation.

Interpersonal Communication Qualities

Even face-to-face communication is often more a simultaneous monologue among several people than a dialogue. Even when there is a genuine effort to understand the other and considerable trust and openness, without appropriate skills, dialogue cannot happen. Here four skills are highlighted: immediacy, concreteness, ownership, and acknowledgment. The discussion is followed by a dialogue demonstrating the use of the skills.

Immediacy. Immediacy refers to the sense of being present, focusing on paying attention, listening, and perceiving the emotional content of messages. In many discussions people are not really present to each other; they are simply waiting for their turn to respond rather than understanding and being responsive.

A successful leader understands that most people have a fairly high need to be really heard and taken seriously. Employees do not want to hear your experiences, to have you fix their problems, or to be treated like a representative of a class of people. They want their feelings and their immediate circumstances responded to. They want understanding and the power to act responsively and responsibly. Interaction characterized by immediacy involves much eye contact and supportive gestures. It is patient and careful and filled with requests for further understanding.

Concreteness. Concreteness refers to expressions that avoid abstractions by providing meaningful details. An expression is abstract whenever it provides a generalized conclusion or evaluation without providing the descriptive information from which such a conclusion or evaluation was reached.

Abstractions create problems because they (a) overgeneralize, making problems appear larger and more difficult to solve; (b) provide listeners with little information on which to base their own evaluations and responses; and (c) tend to evoke responses to the words themselves rather than to what the speaker has actually experienced.

The statement, "John is irresponsible," includes all these qualities. The more concrete statement, "I was disappointed last month when John did not meet his quota," provides a much better opportunity for dialogue, whether the conversation is with John or others.

Concrete expressions help clarify the content of the interaction, provide more and more useful information, reduce emotional intensity, align interpretations, and increase change options. Abstractions are so natural to many people that mutual commitment to exploration and clarification may be necessary for improved communication.

Ownership. Ownership is the process of explicitly assigning and expressing appropriate responsibility for feeling and actions. Unowned statements shift responsibility by taking on too much responsibility or too little, leading to defensiveness, guilt, and inability to correct.

The statement, "You make me so angry," inappropriately shifts responsibility for one's own feelings to the other. Although the other's actions leading to the feelings of anger are important and must be owned by the other, the person feeling anger contributes also. Anger requires both the actions *and* the unmet hopes, desires, expectations, and anticipations of the one having the feeling. Both are appropriately open to discussion.

A lack of ownership is also often present in claims of objectivity and facts. All claims and facts require agreed-on processes or procedures for their formation. Even the accountant's report requires the acceptance of "general accounting procedures" for its claims. Often these processes and procedures remain implicit, making discussion of them impossible and consideration of their products incomplete. Responsibility is pushed to some invisible realm.

Responsibility is also often shifted to rules and generic shoulds and oughts. Questions like "Whose oughts?" "Why are they applicable in this situation?" can be undiscussible. Responsibility is shifted to an absent authority.

Owned messages explicitly demonstrate responsibility for self, thoughts, feelings, knowledge claims, and actions. They often begin with an explicit "I think" or "I want" rather than appearing without an origin. To produce an owned message requires (a) knowing what you are really feeling, thinking, or doing; (b) honestly determining what you have to value, anticipate, or want to think or feel this way when confronted with the other's statements and actions; and (c) determining which are the thoughts and feelings that you wish to share with the other. Most owned statements begin to make explicit the deep values and assumptions that are embedded in an organization's culture.

Acknowledgment. Acknowledgment is the process of making explicit your understanding of the other person's message prior to responding to it. In the absence of acknowledgment the following sequence often results: Important messages from one or both are overlooked, denied, or only partly understood; participants respond to different messages as the interpretations misalign; a bogus issue arises on which the participation partly aligns, thus justifying the heightened emotions; and interactants leave the interaction feeling misunderstood, undervalued, and suspicious.

Acknowledgment can help draw out the underlying interpretations (the right-hand dialogue) that is the real life of interaction and meaning assignment. Acknowledgment increases the possibility of greater understanding, eases distinction between misunderstandings and genuine disagreements, and increases feelings of immediacy and trust. Each participant is affirmed as valued and meanings are clarified.

An Example. Mary is Bill's supervisor. Bill had turned in a lengthy report on a project being considered. Working on it has put him behind on other duties. Mary was quite disappointed with it and still has to prepare her own presentation.

Mary: "Bill, I need you to do that report over."

Bill: "Really?"

Mary: "Yeah, I need it back as soon as possible."

Bill: "What do you want?"

Mary: "More development and more direct answers to their questions."

Bill: "I thought it was pretty good."

Mary: "Well, it doesn't show any drive or initiative—that you have things under control."

Bill: "I know my stuff pretty well."

Mary: "Well, you have to show it if you want to get ahead."

Bill: "For some people, it's all show."

Mary: "I don't make the rules, just get the report in."

The dialogue is not too lengthy or intense but shares characteristics with many attempts at dialogue that fail, often in a much grander way than this one. The interaction grows more difficult and abstract. By the end, little understanding is present, the issues are bigger, neither party feels appreciated, and future interactions are likely to be less frequent and more difficult. Bill does not feel his situation is understood and Mary hides her own frustrations and lack of information in generalizations and blame.

Exercise 5.5

- Identify places in the interaction where the statements lacked immediacy, concreteness, ownership, or acknowledgment.

- Rewrite portions of the interaction demonstrating more productive skills.

The following is a hypothetical rewrite demonstrating interpersonal skills leading to a different end.

Mary: "Bill, John needs more details on projected material costs and time requirements before he can consider approving the project."

Bill: "Ah! I was hoping it was done. I'm so far behind."

Mary: "Yeah, I know you have worked hard on the report at a bad time. But they will meet on Friday. For me to get my part done, I'll need it Thursday afternoon, sooner if possible."

Bill: "You mentioned both the material costs and time requirements. Do you know exactly what they need?"

Mary: "I'm a little frustrated myself. John was not very clear himself. I know they want more on the specific timetable for each phase and some comparative figures for considering suppliers. Maybe we should sit down together and talk it out in detail so that we know what we can say. I'll see if I can find out more."

Bill: "I hope a meeting won't be necessary. I appreciate your help, I want it to go well. I think I know better what is needed, but I may need some help to collect everything before Thursday without messing up the GS project."

Mary: "I know you are pretty pushed, but this is important. I need it to go well, too. Maybe Joe can help on the GS project."

In the rewrite meaningful details are added. Abstract, but concrete-sounding, terms like "do it over," "their questions," "taking initiative," and "showing it" are replaced by details of when and what and by criteria for judgment. Unowned feelings expressed as generic frustration and negative reactions become specified and owned. And each feels better that he or she is understood as explicit attempts are made to play back an understanding of the bases for the feelings and thought of each.

Each of the interpersonal skills is more important when the continued relationship is important, information needs are high, change is desired or occurring, the issues are emotionally laden, or social and cultural differences are great.

An Orientation Toward Collaborative Problem Solving

Most organizations have lots of meetings. Most probably have too many. One of the fears of organizational members as more participative approaches are suggested is that the number of meetings will increase. This need not be the case. In fact, a reduction in the time in meetings is possible.

Most meetings are filled with discussion but not dialogue. Two key characteristics separate discussions from dialogues. First, discussions tend to focus on the airing and advocacy of known positions rather than the exploration of unknown ones. Second, discussions often focus on saying rather than doing. At best they may end with a vote, but often the

TABLE 5.4 Comparison of Adversarial and Collaborative Communication

Adversarial	*Collaborative*
Members are adversaries.	Members are joint problem solvers.
Speaking comes from a position or preferred means of accomplishment.	Speaking comes from an outcome wishing to be accomplished.
Discussion becomes polarized around positions.	Dialogue focuses on complex underlying interests.
Discussion narrows options.	Dialogue broadens field of options.
Facts are used to support positions.	Joint search is used to discover the facts.
Seeks winning arguments.	Seeks workable options.
Problems defined before meeting.	Problems mutually defined in meetings.
Final responsibility for the decision rests on others.	Final responsibility for the decision rests with the group.

SOURCE: Based on Gray (1991, p. 50).

discussion ends with simply the need for more discussion. Dialogue focuses on the reaching of a common understanding and mutual commitment to a decision.

From the standpoint of practice, various forms of collaborative decision making provide the context for dialogue. Collaboration requires a different attitude going into meetings and a different form of interaction in meetings. These differences are well characterized in the differences between adversarial and collaborative communication summarized in Table 5.4.

Exercise 5.6

- Describe a recent conflict situation in an organization with which you are familiar. Identify instances of both adversarial and collaborative communication.

- Think of a situation where two individuals appeared to be fighting over the same resource. Identify why they wanted that resource, or the "end" for which this resource was a "means." Can you identify ways both could simultaneously achieve their ends without using that resource?

▶ Review Questions

▼ Why have more companies turned to increased employee participation in decision making?

▼ What are the differences between governance based on hierarchical control and governance based on participation?

▼ When is employee participation in decision making especially important?

▼ Why might a company chose to involve external stakeholders in decision making?

▼ What are the differences between a mechanistic and an organic conception of empowerment?

▼ Why might greater employee empowerment be of value?

▼ How might organizational members participate in visioning and change processes?

▼ Why would immediacy, concreteness, ownership, and acknowledgment contribute to more productive discussions?

▼ What are the major differences between adversarial and collaborative approaches to discussion and problem solving?

▶ Discussion Questions

▼ What have been your experiences with participation and empowerment programs? When have they succeeded and failed? What might you do about the cynicism that frequently comes with these programs?

▼ Do you feel people can significantly change interpersonal skills and their basic orientations to interaction with others? Under what circumstances are such changes more likely?

▶ References and Recommended Readings

Cooperrider, D., & Srivasta, S. (Eds.). (1990). *Appreciative management and leadership: The power of positive thought and action in organizations.* San Francisco: Jossey-Bass.

Frohman, A. (1997, Winter). Igniting organizational change from below: The power of personal initiative. *Organizational Dynamics*, pp. 39-53.

Gray, B. (1991). *Collaborating: Finding common ground for multiparty problems.* San Francisco: Jossey-Bass.

Harrington-Mackin, D. (1994). *The team building tool kit.* New York: Amacom.

McLagan, P., & Nel, C. (1995). *The age of participation: New governance for the workplace and world.* San Francisco: Barrett-Koehler.

Purser, R., & Cabana, S. (1997, Spring). Using search conferences for planning large-scale strategic change. *Organization Development Journal, 15,* 30-52.

Quinn, R., & Spreitzer, G. (1997, Autumn). The road to empowerment: Seven questions every leader should consider. *Organizational Dynamics,* pp. 37-49.

Senge, P. (1990). *The fifth discipline: The art and practice of the learning organization.* New York: Doubleday.

 # Suggested Case Study

Deetz, S. (1995). Stakeholder representation and building the better mousetrap: The Saturn case." In *Transforming communication, transforming business: Building responsive and responsible workplaces.* Cresskill, NJ: Hampton Press.

6

The Ethics of Cultural Control and Organizational Change

Overview

Managing through a cultural approach provides many important benefits, including high identification, team spirit, coordinated organizational processes, and more widespread and positive participation in decision making. Like all strategies for organizing, however, managing culture and cultural change has significant ethical implications that cannot be overlooked. This chapter explores what it means to be an ethical cultural manager and lays out different ways organizations can plan for and deal with ethical dilemmas stemming from cultural management and change.

The chapter addresses three concerns. First, various organizational structures can lead to unethical activities, and potential dangers reside in cultural control. Second, developing an overall ethics program includes the creation of a formal ethics credo and the maintenance of ongoing programs of ethics. And third, ethical considerations exist in conducting cultural analyses.

Key Objectives of the Chapter

▼ To examine the importance of managing ethics as part of an overall cultural management program

▼ To analyze organizational cultural elements that can lead to unethical activity

▼ To understand the potential dangers of cultural control

▼ To provide guidelines for creating an ethical credo and an ongoing ethics program

▼ To explain the ethical sensitivities of cultural change programs and interventions

▼ To provide an ethical audit designed to help organizational leaders gauge the ethics of cultural management

Questions to Consider

▼ Think of times you have engaged or considered engaging in unethical behaviors, for example, cheating or misrepresentation. To what extent did you take into account the general cultural positions (that is, is cheating common or misrepresentation nearly expected) on these activities in deciding your own course of action?

▼ Have you ever experienced cultural control that was so effective that you rarely thought about how you felt or what you would have preferred? Do you think it is ethical for anyone to control you through controlling how you think and feel?

▼ On what basis do you feel that anyone has a right to inculcate values? Do you believe that ethically positive cultures are a good way to enhance ethical individual choices?

▼ Do you think that some cultures are more ethical than others? How would you assess the relative ethical quality of different cultures?

▼ What are some ethical considerations organizational leaders should think about before engaging in a cultural intervention or change initiative?

▶ **The Need for Ethical Considerations**

Contemporary issues of ethics and socially responsible behavior are complex. Individual and community pressures and ethical directives (or lack thereof) create pressures in organizations. Interconnectedness and interdependency make personal and community standards less useful and less proper. The decline of traditional systems of surveillance and the relativity of certain values in the international context reduce voluntary compliance and increase complexity and uncertainty for organizations. Ethical concerns range from issues of compliance to organizational directives on matters such as expense accounts to complex concerns with human rights, environmental protection, equal opportunity for disadvantaged groups, and fair competition.

These concerns are instantiated in personal activities such as lying on resumes, stealing, and not doing one's job and organizational activities such as using prisoners as workers, moving operations to environmentally less protective communities, offering and taking payoffs and bribes, engaging tax avoidance schemes, creating environmentally unsound or wasteful products or packaging, promoting violent entertainment, adding to the growing income disparity, tolerating sexual harassment, and closing economically successful operations in takeover and merger games.

Organizational cultures have great impact on the way these ethical concerns are addressed. And the attempt to manage the hearts, minds, and souls of organizational members, no matter how useful or important in these situations, has itself deep ethical complications. Many managers promote cultures that are hard on families, the community, and the environment. Despite the opportunity for abuse, leader-induced culture change (especially when combined with widespread participation) can lead to cultures ethically far superior to existing or native cultures. Our concern is how to get there.

Organizational cultures can be conducive to unethical behaviors. In the public context, the effect of culture is sometimes clear. The decision of the Republication Committee to Re-Elect the President to break into the Democratic Party's headquarters in the Watergate Hotel is a classic case of tight culture run astray. The men who made up this committee were intelligent, experienced, and powerful. These qualities did not enable them to see beyond the party line or overcome the paranoia that accompanied that limited vision. Equally clearly, the fund-raising rule stretching and breaking by the Democratic National Committee in 1996 grew out of a lax administration of activities and a culture of "whatever it takes." These two cases illustrate how culture can be party to unethical decisions.

Private sector examples are often more complicated and shielded from public view but no less important. Rarely are they as clear as in the Mitsubishi case where a long-term culture of and acceptance of sexual harassment finally lead to an explosion of lawsuits and public outcry. More often, the rules and the violations are less clear, but they matter both to people in the organization and to those outside.

As we head into the 21st century, organizations are facing a turbulent world of work, with bone-thin budgets, imminent downsizing, global competition, and continual transformation. These situations exacerbate issues of organizational ethics. Employees are feeling greater pressure to perform while using fewer resources in companies that show little commitment to them. Typical studies report that almost 75% of employees perceive pressure to act unethically, and 40%-50% of employees report acting unethically or illegally during any particular year. Common transgressions included cutting corners on quality, covering up illegal incidents, abusing or lying about sick days, deceiving customers, lying to a supervisor or subordinate, and taking credit for another employee's ideas.

Employees are facing this pressure during a time when organizations are becoming more complex and diverse. Globalization provides its own ethical dilemmas. For instance, what is considered to be a gift in one culture might be considered to be a bribe in another. Intellectual property rights are complex, and what might be viewed as collaboration in one country might be seen as stealing another person's idea in an another culture or engaging in unfair competition in yet another.

Because of this and other complexities, organizational leaders clearly need to understand the ethical implications of managing culture and managing through culture. The first question organizational leaders must deal with is, what individual and organizational factors lead to unethical behavior, and how can these factors be managed?

Most organizational ethical codes focus on individual employee behaviors. Ethical credos lay out sanctions against employees who lie, cheat, steal from the company, break the law, or take credit for another person's work. This focus may help individuals to take stock of their personal moral actions. But a fixation on microlevel ethics suggests that all organizational problems can be solved by teaching (or scaring) employees into adopting a moral ethical code. It assumes that everyone faces situations where it is tempting to act unethically and that it is up to the individual to have enough strength and character to stand up and act ethically.

The problem with an exclusively micro view of ethics is that it does little to examine the ways that an organization's cultural strength and character impacts individual employee decisions and activities or the way the organization itself may be operating unethically or socially irresponsibly. Although individual moral codes may be an important part of a culture's ethics, managers must also consider the structures of organizational culture that encourage or are conducive to unethical behavior in a broad sense. Through an incorporation of macroethical issues, cultural managers can encourage ethical values in organizational members through a consideration of cultural structures that impact organizational activity.

▶ Cultural Elements Conducive to Unethical Behavior

Several organizational characteristics can be conducive to unethical behavior. Although managers cannot necessarily prevent the formation of such cultural elements, a simple awareness of their unethical potentiality can curb their power. These situations include work groups that are highly cohesive and closed to outside influences; value statements that are vague, ambiguous, or contradictory; large separations and segmentations between levels of hierarchy or organizational departments; organizational practices that systematically privilege one group of people over another; incentive programs that encourage unfair competition; and a code of silence in regard to organizational ethics.

A Closed, Highly Cohesive System

If an organization is fearful of outside influences or shuts itself off from the organizational environment, members may begin to act unethically. Organizational leaders must know the difference between a strong culture and a culture that encourages groupthink. Groupthink is a phenomenon in which organizational group members become so cohesive that productive conflict or dissent is disallowed. The Watergate incident is a classic example of groupthink.

Although organizational identification is important for a strong culture, organizational leaders can ward off groupthink by encouraging dialogue and dissent. In fact, interpersonal conflict actually improves a group's decision making if the conflict is focused on substantive issues. Therefore, when an organization needs to make an important decision, leaders should invite and welcome diverse opinions and understandings. If a group's decision cannot stand up to environmental or internal scrutiny, then it is most likely neither the most ethical nor the most beneficial course of action for the organization to take.

Vague or Contradictory Vision Statements

As discussed later in this chapter, organizational members rely on ethical credos that follow naturally from their organization's vision and are easy to understand. Unfortunately, many organizations fall into the trap of devising ethical statements that are so vague as to be almost useless. They may include generalities such as, "Employees at our company should treat customers and coemployees fairly and equitably." But what does this mean? When an employee is facing a decision of whether to go over his or her boss's head to report sexual harassment, where should his or her loyalties lie? Who should the employee treat most fairly—the boss or the person who is being harassed?

Sometimes value statements or ethical credos can be self-contradictory. In a public relations company that one of us is familiar with, called P.R. Inc., employees became confused by the company's "Little Instruction Book." The instructions were listed in no particular order and employees did not know which instructions management intended to be highest priority. Simple instructions included "Always turn in projects by deadline" and "Never turn in projects with typos." Sometimes employees were unable to follow both instructions at once—if they were to turn something in by deadline it would include typos, or if they fixed the typos the work could not be submitted by deadline.

Granted, it is difficult if not impossible for value statements to specify the instructions or particular courses of action employees should take in each and every organizational situation. Nevertheless, because value statements by their nature tend to be somewhat vague and priorities can seem contradictory, management must consider ways to make organizational value statements come alive and be practical—an issue that is discussed in more detail later in this chapter.

Excessive Organizational Segmentation

Most organizations are segmented and specialized at least to some extent. Organizations divide both laterally into different departments (e.g., legal, marketing, production) and linearly into different hierarchical levels (e.g., management, middle management, staff). Although some type of segmentation is normal and natural in all organizations, excessive segmentation can make it easier for unethical activities to occur. Organizational departments and power levels must be connected or else it is easy for responsibility to "fall through the cracks."

Large gaps between organizational departments can deter needed lateral communication. Products are often recalled because different departments in the same organization were not well enough linked to discuss safety concerns about a product. For instance, if the marketing department of a toy company is not connected with the production department, it might create a toy that could cause a child to choke. The people in the production department might figure that the toy has already been designed and marketed, so now it is their job to make the toy as it was originally proposed. Just as a secretary might shred papers of unknown origin or a garbage truck driver might dump a load of questionable waste, many people figure that if they are told to do something, then it is their job to do it, no questions asked. Unfortunately, this type of segmentation between departments can allow and encourage smart people to ignore important issues. Unethical behavior by people with very high personal moral codes can result.

Excessive organizational power differences and gaps can also lead to unethical behavior. Studies show that one of the main determining factors of open communication between subordinates and superiors is the subordinates' perceived power difference from the superior. The larger the power difference, the less willing subordinates are to communicate openly with their superior. Therefore, organizations prove to be more open, productive, and ethical when power differences between superiors and subordinates are lessened.

Organizations should also incorporate communication structures between upper management and workers when developing organizational policy. Without clear communication between leaders and members, organizational policies devised by management to be ethical can lead to unethical behavior when carried out by employees. For instance, P.R. Inc.'s instruction "Always turn in projects by deadline" seems to raise few ethical concerns. Management might think twice, however, if they knew that employees often carried out this policy by breaking the law (e.g., speeding down the highway) and lying to clients (e.g., "No sir, we at the agency weren't late. The messenger's car broke down, so it's actually his fault."). Domino's Pizza learned the hard way, through lawsuits, the legal and ethical issues raised by rewarding drivers for quick deliveries.

Incentive Programs Can Encourage Unfair Competition

Most organizations provide incentive programs for employees to motivate or reward them for behaving in the company's best interests. Such programs can take the form of monetary bonuses, end-of-the-quarter vacations, promotions, or simple pats on the back. In the majority of circumstances, these programs do much to help both employees and the organization. Nevertheless, management should beware of incentive programs that encourage unethical or unfair competition between organizational members.

For instance, managers at a Denver-based water treatment company motivated salespeople by offering a one-week luxury vacation to the person with the most water treatment sales each year. This motivation program, in place for years at the company, served to increase employee enthusiasm and boost overall company profits. Near the close of one fiscal year, to increase competition among the salespeople and drive sales, the company's management decided to internally post each employee's sales records. Two salesmen were nearly tied for that year. Driven by the knowledge that he was nearly the vacation winner, the slight underdog sabotaged the other salesman by spreading damaging rumors to his clients and slashing the man's car tires before an important sales call.

This example illustrates an important lesson. Management must be careful of implementing incentive programs that might lead to intense competition and unethical behavior. In this instance, the effect of the incentive program was to encourage unethical behavior that ultimately reduces the company's profits.

Practices That Are Discriminatory to
Certain Organizational Groups

Every organization has practices that are peculiar or specific to its particular goals and values. These practices, which often come in the form of company norms, rituals, and ceremonies, vary from organization to organization. Examples might include the norm that "good" employees stay at work at least until 9 p.m. each night (but do not have to come in until 10:30 a.m. the next morning); weekend work is expected even (or especially) when the deadlines are unrealistic; or employees never go out for meals, except for Thursday night when a group goes out to the local Mexican restaurant. Other organizations hold golf tournaments for their clients, whereas others encourage employees to join the company's softball team.

On their face, all these organizational practices may seem normal, natural, and even fun. On the other hand, these practices can serve to privilege some groups in the organization over others. For instance, it is more difficult for a single parent to work until 9 p.m. or work weekends than it is for a childless person or married person with a stay-at-home spouse. Even if the single parent came in early in the morning to make up the time, it is possible that other employees may still look down on him or her for "always leaving early." Likewise, activities like golf tournaments and softball games can serve as integral networking tools, but such rituals can be problematic if they serve as the only vehicle for associating with a prospective client or the boss.

In the organizational communication classes of one of us, a part-time salesman for a major international hotel chain described how golfing worked at his company. In a discussion of organizational networks, he said, "The main way we get new clients in through golf—how else can you spend three hours with a potential client?" When asked the demographics of the company's sales force, the man said, "It's probably about 60% male, 40% female, and probably about 80% white." When asked the demographics of the company salespeople who attended the golf tournament, the man stumbled, stopped, thought about it for a second, and then said quietly, "Last year, I guess it was all white men . . ."

As this example illustrates, company rituals that may be fun and worthwhile can simultaneously serve to privilege some groups over others. Managers must balance their goals for identification and informal networking opportunities by encouraging varied organizational practices that do not serve to systematically discriminate against a certain group of people.

The Ethics Code of Silence

Human beings learn early in life to keep their mouth shut if they are engaged in "bad" behaviors or associated with "bad" people. As little girls and boys grow up to be organizational members and leaders, this inclination to remain silent about ethical issues continues to prevail. For several reasons very few people talk about ethical problems in public. First, people do not want to implicate themselves. Second, people want to avoid "telling" on their colleagues or clients. Third and most important, people dodge ethical discussion because they are afraid that other people do not share their values. If no one else brings up a certain behavior as unethical, then it seems no one thinks anything is wrong. Protected by a code of silence, unethical actions often are ignored until they become big problems.

As discussed, several organizational structures can lead to an organizational environment or culture that is conducive to unethical behavior. These situations include work groups that are highly cohesive and closed to outside influences; value statements that are vague or contradictory; large separations and segmentations between levels of hierarchy or organizational departments; organizational practices that systematically privilege one group of people over another; incentive programs that encourage unfair competition; and a code of silence about organizational ethics.

Exercise 6.1

● Many service organizations have as one of their main values a focus on the customer. This value often manifests itself in policies such as "Never say no" or "The customer is always right." Could this policy lead to unethical behavior on the part of the employee? How about unethical behavior by the customer? How so?

● If some cultures are more ethical than others, how does this judgment affect the way organizational leaders should approach the merging of two different cultures, especially if they are based in different national cultures? Can one nationality's customs be inherently more ethical than those of another? How do you decide?

▶ Ethical Considerations of Cultural Control

Specific types of ethical dilemmas arise from cultural control. Managing by managing culture is largely focused on integration of organizational goals and values into the lives and choices of members. When members accept these values as their own, they become identified with the organization and make decisions that are in line with the organization's goals. Thus, organizational leaders need not closely supervise employees or inundate them with long lists of rules and regulations.

Cultural control is usually more palatable to employees than bureaucratic or technological control. But the aspect that makes cultural control so effective and well received—its unobtrusive nature—is also what makes it potentially oppressive. Because cultural control is almost invisible, it is difficult for employees to discuss or resist. Therefore, it is important to analyze the ethical implications specific to culture management. Cultural control can be unethical for five main reasons:

1. Organizations may couch participatory or team-based methods as being helpful to organizational members, although the programs are devised by top management to induce higher productivity, efficiency, and increased organizational profits.

2. Employees may control themselves on behalf of management in a way that encourages unfair or unethical practices (such as, in the case of Walmart and Albertson's overtime without pay). In addition, rules that employees devise for themselves may be more rigid than traditional bureaucratic rules devised by management.

3. Cultural control is so strong and effective in large part because employees do not realize they are being controlled. This type of control, if not managed effectively, can obscure and stifle opportunities for resistance, discussion, and change.

4. Organizations that maintain strong cultures are the ones that can be most conducive to unethical behavior (e.g., consider the Watergate example offered in the opening of this chapter). Without proper intervention, strong cultures can harbor groupthink and a gang mentality that can lead to unethical decisions.

5. Cultural management relies on the inculcation of value premises in employees, but this inculcation might lead employees to simply follow organizational rules without contemplating or deliberating on the rules and various ways in which organizational goals should be accomplished.

The preceding situations give rise to "unethical potentialities" of cultural control. Nevertheless, organizational leaders can temper these potentialities. The following section offers several guidelines that can help cultural managers better evaluate the ethics of cultural and unobtrusive control systems. Before beginning the discussion, we should emphasize that organizations are fraught with complexities and practical concerns. The guidelines offered are not rules designed for a simple judgment. Rather, the guidelines serve as ways of considering ethical implications of cultural control programs.

1. Cultural control programs should allow for employee voice—both in devising the program and in offering feedback about the effects of the program. Through participation and the encouragement that employees be involved in organizational decision making, organizational leaders allow for employee feedback. Employee communication about ethics and organizational problems can lead to a healthy, moral organizational atmosphere. Open, reflective communication among organizational members can ward off the dangers (such as groupthink) often associated with strong culture companies.

Research shows that employees often misunderstand organizational ethical mandates, and that even when employees do understand organizational values, they are often unsure how to apply them to everyday practices. Increased communication about ethics (especially when these conversations seem most awkward) is important for clarifying organizational goals and sidestepping misunderstandings.

Organizational leaders should also keep in mind that participatory decision-making programs are most conducive to organizational success when they are fostered—not forced—by management and when employees have the opportunity to voice their concerns about the programs. Employee voice not only can make participatory decision making and cultural control more fair, but it can also increase the chances of organizational survival.

2. Organizations should encourage employee participation in understanding how values differently benefit certain groups in the organization. As discussed in the chapter on framing, savvy organizational leaders know how to couch concepts in a way that is understandable and acceptable to the people they are speaking too. Most managers thus frame their programs in ways that seem to benefit all employees (through, for instance, increased empowerment). Nevertheless, participatory decision-making and cultural control programs are also devised to meet management's goals of increased efficiency, productivity, and profits.

Organizational leaders easily underestimate the ways cultural control programs may be stronger than other forms or control. For instance, employees might actively subjugate themselves to organizational cultural values in a way they would not to more obtrusive bureaucratic rules. Organizations have a responsibility to guard employees against the uncritical acceptance that often accompanies cultural control.

One way to avoid uncritical acceptance is through active "conversation" with employees about organizational issues. To lessen perceived power imbalances between management and workers, organizations enter into dialogues where members discuss a wide variety of questions or issues. Not only can members discuss organizational goals and the means to reach those goals, but they also discuss how those goals privilege one group over another. The aim is not consensus or agreement but ensuring that all voices are heard. Through the voicing of all ideas, organizations can become creative.

Managers might keep in mind Aristotle's "golden mean"—with one end marked by excess and the other marked by deficiency. Excess would refer to organizations only worrying about management goals, and deficiency would refer to organizations not worrying at all about management goals. Of course, organizations must consider productivity, efficiency, and profit, but they should also consider members' voices. Organizational leaders should pursue economic interests while at the same time considering the best social interests.

3. *Organization leaders should encourage subcultural as well as individual creativity and deliberation.* One of the dangers of a strong culture company is that it may not be able to change quickly enough to compete in turbulent environments. Charles Conrad (1993) explains that "strong culture" organizations can encourage people to act unethically. To counteract this ethical dilemma, it is in an organization's best interest to encourage variability, plurality, and creativity in both individual organizational members and organizational subcultures.

Indeed, Aristotle explains in the *Nicomachean Ethics* that individuals are most human when they have free will to deliberate on the different means or alternatives for meeting a certain goal. In other words, people cannot be virtuous or truly human unless they are engaged in choosing the ways they go about meeting goals. Based on this conception, organization leaders must not so thoroughly inculcate organizational values in an individual that the individual does not or cannot engage in deliberation or contemplation. When the power of choice and deliberation are replaced with complete inculcation, employees cannot be full people, because they are engulfed in an environment where choice has no meaning.

4. *Organizations should adopt a situational system of ethics.* Law-based ethical systems are based on creating universal norms without consideration of the context for the law to be exercised. Several organizational scholars have suggested that more situated ethics or ethics based in care are more appropriate to examining the complexities of today's organizational life. In the turbulent world of work, organizational leaders need to "make it up along the way." As organizations head into the 21st century, leaders will need to look around and consider the context before deciding what ought to be done. A situational ethic places communication in the center and considers the idea that an act is good if it probably will result in, or is intended to result in, a balance of good over evil. An ethical stance that considers context may be especially appropriate for cultural managers, because it highlights the importance of relationship.

The preceding four guidelines offer ways for managers to think about the ethical implications of cultural control. As discussed throughout this book, cultural management and control offer many advantages. Members like to feel identified with an organization and therefore generally prefer cultural control over bureaucratic and technological control. Nevertheless, organizational leaders who choose to use cultural management mechanisms and participatory decision-making programs also have a responsibility to organizational members. This responsibility includes allowing for and encouraging member voice and offering forums to discuss organizational goals and who these goals privilege. In doing so, organizations encourage employees to be creative and deliberative— actions that not only guard against homogeneity and groupthink but also encourage employees to think about their choices and thus be "fully human."

Exercise 6.2

● What are some of the potential dangers of cultural control?

● Have you ever been involved in an organization where values were inculcated so thoroughly that organizational members engaged in groupthink? What was the result?

● What are some of the ways that organizational leaders could have warded off the dangers of cultural control?

▶ # Creating an Ethics Program

Despite the unethical potentialities of cultural approaches, organizational leaders should remember that ethics can be positively managed. Organizational leaders can incorporate ethics in their overall cultural management plan. The actions of organizational founders and leaders have a strong influence over employee behavior. By placing ethical considerations on the company's priority list, managers send a direct message that ethical activity is an important organizational value.

Organizational ethics programs are a relatively new occurrence. The practice of ethics training and offering an ethics ombudsman or officer to guide ethics and handle questions began in the early 1980s. According to the Ethics Resource Center, in 1997, 60% of U.S. companies had codes of ethics, and 90% of *Fortune 500* firms trained employees in ethics (Greengard, 1997, p. 44). As we head into the 21st century, visionary organizational leaders are realizing that the creation of ethical programs is an integral part of managing culture.

Creating a vision is imperative to good cultural management. The same holds true for ethics. Anyone who considers a formal ethical vision as window dressing should think of the power and credence given to famous ethical lists such as the Ten Commandments. An ethical credo provides such a vision. Through the creation of an ethics code or credo, both managers and employees are provided with a guide according to which they can understand, direct, and evaluate organizational decisions. Organizational leaders should consider several different factors when devising the ethical credo. Specifically, the credo should (a) parallel the organizational vision, (b) avoid a cookie-cutter approach, (c) be realistic and accessible, and (d) clarify the relations of ethics to the overall company goals or ends.

Parallel the Organizational Vision

Codes of ethics should develop naturally and in parallel form to the organizational vision statement. If the formal organizational vision articulates that employees are the organization's number one resource, then a corresponding ethical credo should emphasize loyalty and preservation of jobs, status, and well-being. On the other hand, if the vision statement articulates an organizational priority of top sales and profits, the ethical credo might do more to accentuate employee actions that place the customer as the number one priority. Leaders should devise the ethical credo to extend and parallel the vision rather than contradict or confuse it.

Avoid a Cookie-Cutter, Simplistic Approach

What should be clear from this discussion is that there can be no one ethical credo that is right for every company. Although most organizational credos illustrate similar elements (including mandates such as "Don't steal" and "Treat other employees with respect"), credos will and should differ based on the organization's particular vision and values. Organizational priorities change from year to year, and a useful code of ethics will shift with the needs of society and the organization.

Organizational leaders should revisit their company's ethics credo at least annually. Through yearly discussions, the credo can be updated to fit changing organizational issues and environments. What might be relevant one year could be defunct the next year, and organizational members often take note of the timeliness of organizational documents as evidence of their importance. If organizational members, for instance, read in the organization's code of conduct, "Employees shall not take office supplies home, including pens, paper, dittos, or typewriter tapes," they will instantly realize that the ethics statement has not been revised since the dawn of computers. And if management does not care about ethics, why should they?

Credos Must Be Accessible, Realistic, and Doable

For ethical credos to have an effect on everyday behaviors, employees need to perceive their contents as realistic and doable. Part of this involves ensuring that credos are accessible to employees. Organizational leaders can do this by placing the credo in visible areas in the organization, such as above the fax machine or in the break room. For instance, Johnson & Johnson lets employees and visitors know how seriously it takes its credo, "Our first responsibility is to those who use our products and services." The credo, carved into a granite block, greets everyone who passes through its main reception area.

Credos should also be simple to remember. As discussed earlier, value statements can never explain the exact actions for every organizational dilemma. In fact, when they are too detailed, such as in the case of P.R. Inc.'s "Little Instruction Book," they can be perceived as self-contradictory. Therefore, organizational leaders should use simple messages that encourage employees to exercise creativity and individuality to reach organizational rules. For instance, messages such as "Remember that our coemployees are just as important as our customers" provide guidance without dictating a specific action (that may be unethical in some contexts). The task of balancing simplicity and specificity is a difficult one. Managers must judge for themselves the degree of specificity that will work best in their particular organization.

Clarify the Means and Ends

One of the most important aspects of an ethical credo is that it emphasizes the company's overall end goals and priorities. Is the overall goal to make a profit for the shareholders? To improve the environment? To please customers? With clear organizational end goals, employees are better apt to understand how to behave along the way. Some organizations have chosen to guide their core ideology in a way that goes beyond just making money.

For instance, Paula Tompkins Pribble (1990) analyzed a Midwestern medical technology firm called BE. Organizational leaders at BE made it clear to employees through the ethical credo and ongoing organizational stories that the company's first priority was "restoring people to full life." Making money, although important, was secondary. Through the continual repetition of this theme, employees learned to behave in ways to achieve the priority of restoring full life. It is important that organizational leaders devise ethical credos in such a way that employees understand organizational priorities and end goals.

In summary, organizational leaders should consider several different guidelines when creating an ethics credo, including that it parallels organizational vision, avoids a cookie-cutter approach, is accessible and realistic, and clarifies organizational means and ends.

Ethical credos serve as a strong base for an ethical culture. Nevertheless, on their own, credos serve as templates. They must be fleshed out with ongoing programs and actions to be practical. Just as the Ten Commandments is contextualized in a long book of stories, organizational ethical rules can only come alive when employees are given the opportunity to discuss the stories and contexts in which ethical considerations come into play.

▶ "Walking the Talk"

James C. Collins and Jerry I. Porras (1994) studied 18 companies to figure out what made them "visionary." According to the authors, these companies had in common leaders who indicated a consistent commitment to an overall organizational identity and value program. An ongoing commitment to ethics can come in a variety of forms. The following section considers these specifications: the inclusion of ethics in organizational socialization programs, ongoing programs that are understandable and fun yet sufficiently complex, implementation of an ethics officer or task force, and organizational structures that motivate employees to act ethically. Just as framing must connect with visioning for the effective management of an overall culture program, cultural leaders need to attend to ongoing practices as well as credos for ethical programs to become a substantive part of the organization.

Including Ethics in the Socialization Process

Employees enter organizations with varying ideas of what is right and wrong and what should be top priority. This variance in values increases when the company employs people from different national cultures. Therefore, it is extremely important that organizations begin to immerse employees in the organization's values immediately on arrival. According to the organizational communication scholars Anne Nicotera and Donald Cushman (1992), who studied ethics programs at GE and IBM, "If the value systems of individuals do not complement the value system of their organization, those individuals will eventually be faced with insoluble ethical dilemmas" (p. 453). Irresolvable dilemmas are not beneficial to either the individual or the organization.

Through socialization programs that are infused with ethical values, new employees are able to understand the priorities of the organization and whether organizational values can mesh with their own. If they do not mesh, employees can make a quick escape, saving themselves and the company problems down the line.

Managers should not only share the formal ethics credo during orientation but supplement the rules and regulations with stories that illustrate classic ways employees have dealt with ethical dilemmas in the past. Leaders can also provide new employees with tokens that illustrate certain ethical values. Ethical reminders such as posters and paperweights might be corny, but they do indicate leadership's values. For instance, at the medical technology company BE, the CEO provided new employees with a medallion in which science and technology were illustrated by an "electrical field raising a modern day Lazarus" (Pribble, 1990, p. 262). This was just one of the ways the BE CEO urged employees to identify with the company's overall ethic of restoring full life.

Making Programs Understandable and Fun, Yet Sufficiently Complex

Good cultural managers understand that creating worthwhile ethical programs is like walking a tightrope. They must balance between the goals of making sure ethics are presented in an understandable and fun manner—but in a way that highlights the complexity of most ethical dilemmas.

One attempt to make ethics simple has already been discussed—P.R. Inc.'s "Little Instruction Book." The book did have the advantages of simplicity and familiarity. Most employees had positive (or at least not negative) feelings toward the popular series, *Life's Little Instruction Book* (Brown, 1991). Modeled after the popular series, P.R. Inc.'s instruc-

TABLE 6.1 Complex Ethical Dilemmas

Hypothetical Questions to Consider

A female applicant holds the perfect credentials to become our company's new international trademark attorney. Unfortunately, company executives are concerned that overseas strategic alliances will not take a female attorney seriously and therefore will refuse to work with us. What do we do?

Our company has been plagued with overtime for the past 3 weeks and the vice president has promised employees that they will not have to work overtime in the next month. Because of the overtime, employees are behind on current client work, and we have promised a long-term client that we will finish her long-overdue media campaign within the week. At the last minute, the company learns of a new business opportunity that could net the company hundreds of thousands of dollars. Work needs to be completed by the end of the week. As the vice president, what do you do?

A customer asks an employee for the company's product but cannot afford to buy it at the company's prices. From a past job, the employee knows how the customer could get the product at a cheaper price. What should the employee do?

---

tions were listed simply and acontextually. One was listed every day on the employee's daily newsletter. Although this provided ethical mandates in easy-to-swallow bite-size pieces, it unfortunately did not provide a context for instructions. The program was easy to understand and familiar, but it may have been so simple so as to be defunct.

Ethical programs must go beyond simple acontextual instructions. Employees do not want to feel that ethical programs insult their intelligence, and obvious rules such as "Don't steal" or "Don't lie" can do so. One way to remedy such a problem is to incorporate case study analyses of ethical dilemmas as part of an ongoing ethical program. Possible dilemmas could include those illustrated in Table 6.1. Complex ethical questions invite discussion and deliberation. Organizational leaders should allow members to creatively think about these situations. After in-depth deliberation leaders can offer their own opinion of the situation, while continuing to emphasize that complex ethical dilemmas rarely have a single "right" answer.

Implementation of an Ethics Officer or Task Force

The single largest predictor of a successful ethics program is buy-in and visible support from top management. Charismatic organizational leaders have a tremendous impact on the ways organizational members think and behave and this cannot be ignored in the implementation of an ethics program. When top management makes ethics a visible priority, other employees are more likely to consider ethical implications in their everyday decision making. In addition to behaving in an ethical manner themselves, managers can indicate ethical involvement a couple of different ways.

First, organizations can appoint an ethics officer or ombudsman. The person in this position ensures that the organization's ethical systems are functioning. He or she is involved in ethics training, both during orientation and through ongoing programs. This person also provides guidance to employees experiencing ethical dilemmas and serves as a contact person for employees to report suspected wrongdoing. The ethics officer should encourage open and honest communication from employees and be discreet with information provided.

Second, organizations can implement an ethics committee to oversee, interpret, and continually revise and update the organization's code of ethics. Early in the ethics initiative, this committee can form the ethical program or code it will eventually look after. This committee is also often in charge of deliberating on information received from the ethics officer about misconduct in the organization.

Through the implementation of highly visible positions, where the sole or main priority is to implement ethics training programs and help organizational members with ethical dilemmas, employees are continually reminded of the importance of ethics in the organization.

Organizational Structures That Motivate Employees to Act Ethically

Employees work to receive rewards. The type of rewards desired range from monetary compensation and promotions to relationships and praise. It makes sense that employees are more likely to act ethically when doing so simultaneously helps them achieve the rewards they strive for. Therefore, managers must ensure that organizational structures reinforce ethical behavior on a daily basis.

For instance, bonuses, raises, and promotions should consider the ethical actions of employees. Simply including ethical considerations as a section in employee evaluations can provide an important reminder that organizations take ethics seriously. Because actions speak louder than words, organizational leaders need to walk their talk. If an employee acts unethically—especially if this employee is of high rank or visibility—other employees will pay attention to how the organization deals with the wrongdoer. The management consultant Peter Robertson recently noted, "I know an executive vice-president who got fired for sexual harassment. . . . [The company] didn't have to do a lot of training after that" (Sixel, 1996, as cited in Conrad & Poole, 1998, p. 388). Actions speak louder than words.

The real issue is credibility. If organizational structures are not put into place that reward ethical activity and punish unethical actions, then the ethical credo remains only words on paper. Likewise, if the ethical officer or ethics committee consists of low-power, underrespected personnel, then other organizational members are unlikely to take ethics seriously. Obviously, organizations must pick and choose where they will expend energy and place their best and brightest employees. Just as with any other set of cultural values, by remembering the important interplay between visioning and framing, organizational leaders can implement an effective ethics program.

Exercise 6.3

Read carefully the following case based on Carey (1998, p. 57):

Lockheed Martin, a large Maryland-based manufacturing company, has found a creative and fun way to include ethics in ongoing management training. Based on Scott Adams's popular cartoon *Dilbert*, employees have learned about ethics through a humorous, interactive board game called "The Ethics Challenge." The game, which was played by all 175,000 Lockheed employees in 1997, presents hypothetical ethical dilemmas that employees must deliberate on. Employees must choose one of four possible responses. The creativity and humor of the game derive from the cartoon's characters, who provide the responses.

Dogbert, the "evil human resources director," always provides a funny or cynical response. His response often represents what many employees might think but not have the gumption to say. Through this approach, everyone can laugh and feel comfortable and then get into a more serious discussion about how they would approach the situation.

The game was introduced in late 1996 in a management training session. In the early months of 1997, Lockheed employees around the nation got wind of the game and started calling headquarters to find out when they could play. Headquarters was amazed that employees were actually asking for their ethics training. Another advantage of the game was that it required virtually no training. Employees only needed to watch a 6-minute video on the rules of the game, hosted by senior management and Dogbert.

Did it work? According to an internal Lockheed survey conducted after the implementation of the game, employees cited improvement in the involvement of immediate supervisors in helping subordinates who spoke with them about ethical dilemmas. Since the implementation of "The Ethics Challenge," Lockheed has provided the game to more than 1,500 corporations and educational groups.

- What are some of the advantages of "The Ethics Challenge?"

- Keeping in mind the guidelines offered in this chapter, what would you say made the game work?

- Can you foresee any dangers with the use of such a game for ethics training? If so, what are they? How could management overcome these dangers?

- Do you think that the game will be just as effective at organizations other than Lockheed? Why or why not?

▶ Ethical Considerations of
Cultural Change

Cultural managers should also consider the potential ethical problems of conducting a cultural analysis. Study and intervention have direct effects on people's lives. Neutrality or certainty are never possible. Edwin Schein (1992) identifies two main risks of cultural interventions.

The Analysis of the Culture Might Be Incorrect

Whenever a person attempts to describe an organization's culture, he or she runs the risk of simply being wrong. If decisions are made on incorrect evaluations of the organization's culture, serious harm could be done. Errors are most likely to be due to an incomplete analysis that relies too heavily on official organizational documents and espoused values. Cultural analysts should remember that everyday behavior is just as important, if not more important, in creating and sustaining organizational culture as formal mission statements and ethical credos. Therefore, analysts should be wary of offering advice based solely on organizational documents and interviews with top-level management. Analysts can incorporate considerations of values-in-use through observing day-to-day activities and interviewing employees from all levels in the organization.

Organizational Members May Not Be Ready for the Analysis

Often, organizational leaders give little forethought to how they are going to use the information derived from a cultural analysis of their organization. Just as therapy can reveal things to an individual that are painful, organizational culture analyses can provide information that is not easy for organizational members to hear. Therefore, cultural analysts must go beyond dropping their cultural analyses in employees' in boxes. They should also consider providing recommendations for employees about how they can best understand and make sense of the information, especially if the information is negative, surprising, or depressing. In agreeing to perform a cultural analysis, the cultural analyst simultaneously takes on the responsibility for dealing with the consequences of such an intervention.

Being an ethical leader in today's organizations is a difficult process. It means going beyond living up to one's own moral code to maintaining an organizational culture that motivates and rewards ethical behavior from all employees. Managers can be reassured in knowing that ethics has its advantages. Ethical employees tend to outperform others, selling more products and receiving fewer complaints. Employees also tend to be more accountable in an ethical culture and take responsibility for mistakes. Finally, an ethical organization tends to be more predictable and calm because employees feel free to address ethical concerns as they arise rather than allowing them to turn into long-term problems. Maintaining an ethical organization, however difficult, pays off in the end.

Based on the preceding discussion of the dangers of cultural control, the steps to creating an ethics program, and ethical considerations of change and analysis initiatives, the following list of questions makes up an ethical audit for cultural managers. Like all such lists, this audit is most useful when it is adapted to fit the specific organization and accompanied by a contextualized discussion of typical ethical dilemmas. The audit is designed to serve as a base from which cultural managers can gauge ethics in their organizations.

Organizational leaders who wish to manage culture in an ethical manner should work toward programs that would allow them to answer "Yes" to the following 24 questions.

An Ethical Audit

1. Do leaders consider both organizational structures and individual behaviors that lead to unethical activity?

2. Are organizational decisions held up to environmental scrutiny and do leaders invite internal as well as external dissent?

3. Are value statements clear and noncontradictory?

4. Are structures in place that facilitate interdepartmental communication?

5. Are structures in place that deter excessive power differences between supervisors and subordinates?

6. Are structures in place that deter unfair employee competition?

7. Does the organization balance its practices and rituals so they do not systematically discriminate against a certain group of people?

8. Do leaders encourage ethical discussion and deliberation?

9. Do leaders allow for open forums where employees can discuss the implications and dangers of cultural control?

10. Do organizational programs encourage individual and subcultural creativity?

11. Does the credo encourage organizational members to consider the culture's context when making an ethical decision?

12. Is the ethical credo derived from the overall organizational vision?

13. Do organizational leaders allow for, listen to, and incorporate employee voice in developing the credo?

14. Is the credo understandable and realistic, yet not overly simplistic?

15. Does the credo go beyond emphasizing the short term and obvious?

16. Does the credo allow for self-reflection and discussion?

17. Does the credo clarify overall end goals of the organization?

18. Are organizational leaders walking their talk?

19. Are ethical values communicated to employees in a fun, yet sufficiently complex, manner?

20. Is a formal ethics officer or task force developed in the organization?

21. Are ethics infused into the organization's socialization program?

22. Are organizational structures built in to reward ethical actions and sanction unethical action?

23. Have organizational leaders considered the implications of conducting an ethical analysis?

24. Are organizational leaders prepared for common reactions people have toward organizational change?

 Review Questions

▼ What are some of the organizational cultural elements that are conducive to unethical behavior?

▼ Cultural control has several dangers. What are they? What can managers do to overcome these potential problems?

▼ What are some guidelines managers can consider when devising an ethical credo?

▼ How can organizational leaders make their ethical values come alive through ongoing programs and organizational structures?

▼ Why must managers be aware of ethics when conducting a cultural intervention or change initiative?

▶ Discussion Questions

▼ Can seemingly harmless organizational rituals, such as the company golf game, serve to systematically privilege some organizational groups? Is it possible for organizational leaders to prevent systematic privilege? If so, how?

▼ What are some specific ethical considerations managers should keep in mind when managing a diverse workforce? How does globalization affect the way ethical credos and programs are designed and implemented?

▼ Have you ever been involved in designing or implementing an ethical program? If so, what were some of the challenges to doing so? How were these challenges met?

▼ Have you been aware of ethics programs being in place at organizations where you have worked? If so, were they taken seriously? Why or why not?

▶ References and Recommended Readings

Brown, H. J., Jr. (1991). *Life's little instruction book.* Nashville, TN: Rutledge Hill Press.
Carey, R. (1998, April). The ethics challenge. *Successful Meetings, 47,* 57.
Collins, J., & Porras, J. (1994). *Built to last: Successful habits of visionary companies.* New York: HarperCollins.
Conrad, C. (1993). *The ethical nexus.* Norwood, NJ: Ablex.
Conrad, C., & Poole, M. S. (1998). *Strategic organizational communication: Into the twenty-first century* (4th ed.). Fort Worth, TX: Harcourt Brace.
Deetz, S., Cohen, D., & Edley, P. (1997). Toward a dialogic ethics in the context of international business. In F. Casmir (ed.), *Ethics in international and intercultural communication.* Hillsdale, NJ: Lawrence Erlbaum.
Greengard, S. (1997, October). 50% of your employees are lying, cheating & stealing. *Workforce, 76*(10), 44-53.
Nicotera, A., & Cushman, D. (1992). Organizational ethics: A within-organization view. *Journal of Applied Communication Research, 20,* 437-463.
Pribble, P. T. (1990). Making an ethical commitment: A rhetorical case study of organizational socialization. *Communication Quarterly, 38,* 255-267.
Schein, E. (1992). *Organizational culture and leadership* (2nd ed.). San Francisco: Jossey-Bass.
Seeger, M. (1997). *Ethics and organizational communication.* Cresskill, NJ: Hampton Press.

Culture and
Technological Change

Technology is a central feature of many organizations today. New technologies are frequently implemented to increase efficiency, enhance productivity, and improve profitability. Although the most common way to think about technology today focuses our attention on communication and information technologies, technology can involve the implementation of any tool system that alters the way work is done.

For implementing new technological systems in an organization, several factors bear consideration. Technology inevitably has an effect on the organizational culture by affecting the ways in which organizational members must interact with one another to accomplish routine tasks. Before ascertaining how the implementation of new technology may impact the organizational culture, developing a clear sense of the ways different processes become interrelated can be helpful. Once new systems take hold in an organization, the structure of power relationships may be fundamentally altered, and culture may be affected as various organizational dynamics change the way members think about and make sense of their organizational experience.

For these reasons, several central questions should be asked regarding the organizational impact of technological changes. This chapter explores the issues surrounding the implementation of new technological systems and probes how such change may impact the organization at a deeper level. The suggested case study illustrates some of these issues as they have played out in context.

Key Objectives of the Chapter

▼ To aid in identifying the multiple ways in which technological change may impact an organization

▼ To increase understanding of how technology may affect common work practices in the organization

▼ To increase understanding of the influence of cultures on the understanding of information and role of information technologies

▼ To explain the impact of information technologies on power and knowledge dynamics in the organization

▼ To aid the management of culture through technological change

▼ To aid leaders' ability to identify who will be most directly affected by any technologically induced changes that occur

▼ To develop skills in implementing technological changes to complement rather than disrupt functional systems in the organization

Questions to Consider

▼ What business processes can be enhanced by technological change?

▼ What cultural systems are embedded in the current processes?

▼ How can technology complement cultural systems?

▼ In what ways might such changes create tensions or problems in the organization?

▼ What evidence have you seen of resistance to technological innovations? How much of this resistance is grounded in cultural features, underlying values, or assumptions about people and the work process?

▶ How Are Technology and Culture Related?

In every organization, the routine processes required to accomplish day-to-day tasks organize behavior and interaction in certain ways. The nature of that interaction helps shape the way organizational members think about the work that they do and how they come to understand what organizational managers value. The use of technology in the workplace directly affects how knowledge about work is communicated. Whether the tools in question are information technology (IT) per se or not, information about one's work gets conveyed in the processes required to carry out day-to-day tasks.

Technology is often thought of as complex, intricate, and hard to understand. Although this is sometimes true, for the purposes here technology is thought of as any tool or resource that is used to transform organizational inputs to outputs. Thus, technology can be as simple as a pen and paper or as complex as a state-of-the-art worldwide cellular access system. Each shapes practices and each shapes culture.

In regard to communication technologies, organizational culture is influenced by the ways in which organizational members receive information and store knowledge about their jobs. Technological impact is never simple nor even. Subcultures in an organization use technologies differently in the accomplishment of their tasks and are oriented differently toward IT and its usefulness.

Carole Groleau and James Taylor (1996) provide a useful study of technological changes in the purchasing process at a large organization that demonstrate how a failure to account for the embedded nature of work processes in organizational life can lead to their ineffective implementation. Their study tracked the process of computerization in the purchasing department at a "crown corporation." Prior to computerization both agents and clerks used paper documentation to complete the entire purchasing process from the initial purchase request, through the bidding process, to the final purchase. This process provided written documentation of all the steps along the way but took a great deal of time.

To increase productivity, the corporation computerized this process so that all documentation was stored electronically. What the corporation failed to account for, however, was the quality of information that was accessible to organizational members all along the way under the old system. Under the new system the same data were available but had become "segmented" into different screens and formats that made it difficult to access all the information at once. By removing decisions at different stages of the process from the context of prior decisions, organizational members found their tasks complicated. This case illustrates nicely how technology may complicate organizational activity if management does not account for the way that an organizational task structures organizational activity and is worth reading.

In an era where organizational problems are often addressed with "upgrades," developing a mechanism for more broadly assessing the usefulness of technological systems in performing specific operations may help open alternatives. When changes are implemented, such implementation generally falls to leaders in the organization. For this reason, a clear sense of how technological changes may impact current systems and be appropriated by organizational members will help ease the transition for those who will be responsible for day-to-day interaction with the modified systems.

▶ What Counts as Information?

Although appearing straightforward, the question of what counts as information may in fact be answered very differently depending on one's cultural perspective. This clash can lead to problems in an organization when those individuals responsible for making productivity assessments and designing or implementing technological change respond differently to this question than those who will ultimately be responsible for integrating such change into their work activities.

Workers responsible for the development of information technology may have a propensity for viewing information as data. Following from this perspective, information can be stored, divided, transmitted, reassembled, and analyzed. If information is no more than quantifiable bits of data then its context is not important to its use. This perspective is important to individuals who must devise mechanisms for rapid storage and retrieval of data, and it shapes the way technology is designed. This is not the only way that it can be designed, but it has been the norm.

Those who must use information on a daily basis to make decisions, however, may encounter frustration as decisions that have evaluative consequences have to be made based on data that have been stripped of

TABLE 7.1 Assumption About Information: IT Professionals and Others

IT Culture Assumptions About Information	Alternative Conceptualizations
Information can be accurately digitized and transmitted electronically.	This process only captures data; information must be gained by other interpretive processes.
Information can be broken into pieces for convenient storage and retrieval.	Information is only useful when contextualized and evaluated as part of holistic systems.
Information can be viewed as snapshots on screen or in printed form.	Information is in constant flux; fixing it fundamentally alters its nature.
Faster is better.	Speed may reduce the quality of decisions made.
More is better.	Too much of the wrong kind of information wastes time and leads to less effective decisions.
Quantifiable information leads to reliable and consistent decisions.	Much information must be viewed in qualitative form to be able to make useful and just decisions.
The less paper used the more efficient the system.	Some tasks are done better by handling paper.

SOURCE: Based on Schein (1992, p. 280).

their qualitative nature. The information required to make many decisions needs to be contextualized for employees to be assured that they are making an accurate assessment of a situation.

Before exploring the many ways technology may impact organizational culture and structures, it is perhaps useful to examine the different cultural assumptions that are embedded in the approach to information technology itself. Edwin Schein (1992) has outlined several assumptions that information systems (IS) designers frequently have for information. This has also allowed him to point to alternative ways of conceptualizing information that may lead to alternative conceptions of technological change. Table 7.1 summarizes these concepts.

Viewing the introduction of information technologies, as many IT and management information systems (MIS) people do, as simply an improvement of efficiency overlooks the effects of technologies on power relations, work practices, and values. Hence, resistance is misunderstood or simply written off as antiprogress or technophobia.

▶ Identifying Goals of Technological Change

As Groleau and Taylor (1996) illustrate, sets of decision-making processes are often interrelated in organizational systems, and encountering
circumstances in which one is not aware of the context of prior decisions
may make later decisions more difficult. If processes are breaking down
in an organizational system, before considering implementing technological changes to resolve them, organizational leaders should develop
a deeper understanding of their nature. Doing so may help in understanding (a) whether technology can actually resolve the problem at
hand, and (b) what factors about functional aspects of current processes
will need to be taken into consideration in designing an intervention to
adequately and appropriately address the problems.

When considering changes that will affect the way routine practices
are carried out in the organization, it is important to consider the rami-
fications of those changes. Identify what goal your organization seeks to
accomplish by altering existing processes and then attempt to ascertain
how those changes will affect the broader culture.

If, for example, the goal is to increase production speed or output
volume, assess what may be gained by the time currently involved in the
process or the speed at which items are currently produced. Will there
be a qualitative change in the process incurred by changing it? Groleau
and Taylor (1996) demonstrate that after computerized mechanisms for
generating purchase orders were implemented, the advantages and disadvantages incurred were not necessarily those that had been expected.
Although the actual time to print was decreased, the organizational
members' degree of familiarity with the cases and subsequent ability to
answer customer inquiries was significantly reduced. Similarly, the ability of an organizational member to easily assess what had taken place at
different stages of the decision-making process was inhibited by the format in which the information was now accessible.

If the goal of technological change is to increase member access to
multiple sources of data pertaining to a given decision issue, consideration must be given to the way data are presented in the new form. It
may make intuitive sense that employees who can access information
directly from their desktop terminals can save time by not having to find
files of certain information. But if the information is not available in a
manner in which different pieces of information can easily be compared
and evaluated simultaneously, then the time saved in one area may be

lost in another. This may happen when employees are forced to flip between screens or find themselves having to print information from various sources and resort to comparing printed versions.

▶ Assessing the Potential Impact of Technological Change on Culture

All of the factors discussed in the previous section impact the larger organizational culture in many ways. Dealing with technological change is an issue that has always faced businesses. First, the ways in which employees gain knowledge about the tasks that they perform directly affects their understanding of their role in the organization.

Whenever new tools are introduced, the experience of tasks changes. In manufacturing arenas, the gradual shift to increased levels of automation not only changed the types of tasks required of employees but also changed what types of knowledge were considered valuable by the organization and thus affected how decisions were made. Where mechanical equipment once required expert laborers to run and maintain it, advanced computer systems now perform many of the same tasks. As this shift took place, the bodily experience of working on the shop floor changed. Machines now required little regular handling. On one level, this transformation allowed for increased consistency and controls to be implemented. On the other hand, skilled laborers who had performed certain operations for years found themselves either unnecessary or forced to interact with familiar systems in unfamiliar ways.

Oversight of operations has also become more centralized, taking place in a control room filled with computer screens and display mechanisms rather than on the factory floor. Several accounts describe the discomfort experienced by many workers, accustomed to identifying trouble based on sounds, smells, and visceral experience with tangible equipment, but now expected to trust a series of numbers, dials, buttons, and warning lights.

The case study of computerization in the purchasing department (Groleau & Taylor, 1996) also indicates that learning to trust decontextualized data when one has become accustomed to making decisions at a more qualitative level is unsettling for many. For an organizational leader, understanding the root of this discomfort can assist in the introduction of technological change.

Identifying Technological Impact on Common Work Practices

There is no inherent value in change. A problem with the status quo may suggest a fine-tuning of current processes or increases in resources available to carry out those tasks, but often the first impulse is to find a better way. The scenarios referred to above point to ways in which change can lead to breakdowns in current systems or strip current processes of valuable attributes. Frequently, such system breakdowns occur when the variable contributions made by the individuals in the process are not adequately accounted for.

Again, this conceptualization can be traced back to different perceptions of what counts as information. In developing information technology or automating mechanical systems, those responsible for research and development often begin by observing current work practices and attempting to develop a schema for how various tasks are performed. By breaking complex tasks down into component parts, job activities can be quantified, analyzed, and transformed into the mathematical equations that drive most technological systems. Problems arise when the subtleties of decision-making processes at points of human interface are neglected or underestimated.

If a systems analysis only indicates that certain pieces of information must travel in certain ways between various departments, then programs can be written that permit such transfers to take place more rapidly via electronic means. When such programming fails to account for the way in which that information is handled by various individuals in those different departments, however, or precludes the handling of information in particular ways, the transfer of data may fundamentally alter the experience of information for the organizational members responsible for making decisions.

The way organizational members experience their value to the organization and how they perceive their role in performing essential tasks for the organization directly affects their identification with the company. Because of this, ensuring that technological change does not negatively impact on employees' abilities to adequately perform their tasks is particularly important to maintaining strong cultural identification.

Just as it is important to get input from organizational members and stakeholders at other key decision points, enlisting their help in identifying appropriate technological changes can be crucial to success. Often, they have a greater understanding of the intricacies of day-to-day practices with which they are intimately involved. Through their insight into both what works well and what poses difficulties under the current system, a clearer sense can emerge of where to target change efforts.

The Impact of Technological Change on Organizational Structure

Just as technological change affects day-to-day operations in existing organizational structures, it also alters those structures or gives rise to new ones. In the manufacturing example referred to above, the individuals whose knowledge was most valued in the organization shifted dramatically after automation occurred. Whereas earlier systems had required the knowledge of skilled labor to maintain the smooth operation of equipment, automated systems required instead a certain degree of comfort with information technology, a degree of mathematical skill to interpret data readouts, and a willingness to trust the new way information was being presented. Often, those best suited to performing well under earlier systems have great difficulty accommodating to new mechanisms.

This type of transition can become difficult for an organization to negotiate for several reasons. First, those now best equipped to handle new technology often may have significantly less experience in the organization. Those who may rapidly become responsible for performing tasks vital to the organization's functioning may either have relatively little seniority or be new hires, trained explicitly to be able to operate the automated systems. Having little familiarity with actual operations on the floor gives newcomers little context in which to frame their understanding of the function of the tasks they will perform. Similarly, when automation breaks down, these individuals may be poorly equipped to diagnose and repair malfunctions on the floor.

In organizations where technological change is more informational, structural changes may be felt also. The case study exemplifies one way this happens when organizational members no longer have direct access to information in a form that permits them to easily perform the mundane tasks required by their job.

At a more macro level, however, upper management identifies itself by the quality of the work performed. Generally decisions made at higher levels of the organization are less cut-and-dried, require more flexibility, and are more intuitive. As technology is implemented that strips down decisions to strict equations and eliminates intuitive input, these tasks tend to get pushed down the hierarchy. On the one hand, managers may be pleased to have their time freed to perform other tasks. On the other hand, they may find that a lack of direct involvement in the decision-making processes at other levels affects the degree to which they are in touch with day-to-day activities of the organization.

As practices originally performed at certain levels of the organization get moved around or performed differently, an assessment must be made regarding the qualitative outcomes of the decisions made under the new systems. There are certainly situations in which technological innovation can enhance individuals' capacity to perform their job well. Since this is not always the case, however, being able to assess early on how change may fundamentally impact your organization's ability to make informed decisions and deliver quality products or services can be helpful in developing systems that most comfortably complement your organizational culture and existing systems.

Exercise 7.1

The following questions can provide a useful starting point for considering how organizations handle information exchange and how intrusion into those systems may enhance or detract from its ability to achieve its goals. To answer these questions, think specifically of an organization that you are familiar with that is experiencing difficulties. Try to focus on a specific section or unit in that organization.

* What information does the unit need to perform its job?
* How does that information get shared with other units?
* What else is gained by the mechanism through which information is transmitted?
* How do current information systems shape the way members think about and understand their role?
* What relationships are developed and maintained through the transmission of information?

- What benefits do organizational members derive from developing those relationships?

- Does handling information pertaining to one task affect one's ability to perform another?

- How is information distributed across levels of the organization?

- What types of power are associated with the handling and processing of certain information?

- Would organizational dynamics change if this information was distributed differently?

- What qualities of current systems are important to preserve as change is considered?

- Who will be most directly affected by these changes?

- How should those affected be involved in the development of alternatives?

Assessing the Effect of Change on Power and Knowledge Structures

The questions in Exercise 7.1 can help bring attention to the underlying power and knowledge structures in your organization and how they are created and maintained in large part based on the access that employees have to information. The degree to which one understands how different processes work in an organization and how access to critical information generally shapes the degree of a person's power and influence in an organization.

Often, new technological systems are implemented with the intention of flattening hierarchies and distributing authority and responsibility more evenly throughout the organization. Although often a means to achieving better decisions and increasing the identification of organizational members, such reorganization typically redistributes power in certain ways. Understanding both the potential gains and the challenges that may be encountered is important before beginning such an undertaking.

As systems of power and knowledge are reconfigured, it is possible that organizational members will be able to use their new autonomy to identify and respond to localized problems before these become severe. They may be able to develop adaptive systems for handling the situations for which they have become responsible. This presumes, however, that the reorganization has simply shifted responsibility for certain tasks to different sections of the organization. What might the results be, however, if the flattening of hierarchy simultaneously diffuses responsibility? As reorganization takes place, considering where the "buck stops" for different tasks is important. Do those who will now ultimately be responsible for certain decision outcomes accept and welcome that responsibility? Do they see the relevance of those decision outcomes to organizational goals? Are they rewarded for their decision-making efforts?

This scenario again presumes, however, that the hierarchy remains fundamentally intact but responsibilities are shifted. Think of an organization of which you are a member. How does this organization depend on its hierarchical structure for identity? What modifications would be likely to take place if titles—and positions—carried less prestige or were eliminated in favor of other systems? Considering how the organization would be affected by such changes can help organizational leaders to determine what benefits their organization might gain from reconfiguration and help them to be attentive to potential challenges that might be encountered in the transition process.

▶ The Influence of Cultural Identification on Adaptability

The extent to which changes are welcomed in a given organization depends a great deal on the degree and nature of member identification with the organization. This includes members at all levels of the hierarchy. Change is likely to fundamentally alter the nature of interaction in the workplace. To be receptive to change, members must understand their role in the fulfillment of a larger purpose and see how change will better enable them to accomplish organizational goals.

For members with less power under current systems, change may involve increased responsibility, alter the nature of interpersonal relationships they have with coworkers, or affect the way that they must interact physically with their task to execute it. For a member who is not identified with the vision of the organization, change may be felt as an added burden.

Members who have high identification with the organization, however, derive pleasure from the outcome of their task performance because they see its relationship to the fulfillment of a larger purpose. To help develop this identification, managers will have taken the perspectives of various stakeholders into account when developing plans for change. They will also have clearly communicated to those who will be affected by the change both how their new roles will be important to the organization and how they will benefit from and be compensated for their increased responsibilities.

Members who currently hold greater power in the organization may have worked hard to gain the power and prestige that currently accompanies their position. Many years of long hours and other sacrifices may have been made to advance their careers. If implementation of technological change is aimed at flattening hierarchy, redistributing power, or increasing worker autonomy, middle managers, in particular, but also management in general, may have occasion to question their role in the new system. If those they traditionally were responsible for directing and supervising now have the ability and authority to make many of those decisions on their own, what would managers' new roles be? Would their positions hold less prestige? Would they still be necessary to the organization? How would the salary structure change as power and authority are disbursed?

Again, managers who do not see their role in the fulfillment of a larger organizational purpose may feel anxiety. For those, however, who have a broader vision for the organization's future, it will generally be easier to see how change does or does not help to move the organization toward that future. As these are the people who will generally be most closely involved in development plans, it will be especially important for them to see the function of these changes in advancing the needs of the organization. Leadership will be responsible for not only implementing changes but often also for training organizational members to perform new tasks and evaluating the effectiveness of new processes during periodic reviews. Managers having a clear sense of why such changes are beneficial to the organization will help give focus to these tasks. If such awareness does not exist, it is perhaps a good idea to revisit the usefulness of implementing change at all.

▶ **Assessing the Usefulness of Technological Change**

As an organization moves forward toward the accomplishment of various goals, members will experience setbacks and stumbling blocks. When this happens, it will be important to be able to determine what types of modifications are necessary to restore focus and help the organization get back on track. Working through some of the scenarios above can help management focus on potential areas of concern. Assessing the situation and asking specific types of questions can be useful also. There is no fixed formula or set of questions that can be universally applied across all organizations. There are genres of problems that one is likely to encounter, however, and the following models may be used to spur thinking and develop questions specific to your own organizational circumstances.

Where Is Breakdown Occurring?

Clearly identifying the source of the problem will help save the organization valuable time and resources by avoiding Band-Aid approaches to problem solving. Clearly identifying how and why current systems are failing to move the organization toward desired goals is one way of determining whether the type of change required is one of repair or of transformation. Before large amounts of capital are invested in technological solutions, gaining a sense of how current processes function will help in assessing whether minor modifications in current systems can remedy the situation or whether more systematic change is necessary.

Taking the time to engage in this process can be beneficial for several reasons. First, it allows simple problems to be addressed with simple solutions. Second, if the problems are more complex or if the general consensus across organizational levels indicates that a technological change may be beneficial, a deeper understanding of the cultural context in which those systems are embedded will have already been developed. This understanding will then enable a more sophisticated analysis of what types of change may be most useful once it has been determined that change is, in fact, necessary.

Who Will Be Affected by These Changes?

After a determination of whether or not change is necessary, it is important to identify who will be most directly impacted by the changes that occur. Having assessed the nature of the breakdown also positions you nicely to be able to make this evaluation. Knowing who currently has responsibility for certain processes will aid in the identification of individuals whose jobs may change as systems are altered.

In making such an assessment, consideration of how information gets disseminated among and between organizational members as well as how access to that information shapes and defines power relationships will be important. Any members who are identified as potentially being impacted by technological change should be considered stakeholders in the process and should be involved in regular dialogue as change processes are developed.

How Will These Changes Affect Them?

Before any changes are implemented, every attempt should be made to assess how organizational members will be impacted by the changes. In doing so, attention to levels of identification will help pinpoint potential sites of resistance. Areas in which potential resistance is identified should be given particular attention and members invited to collaborate in the development of change systems. Resistance to change is not always an indication of stubbornness. Sometimes organizational members who deal with particular processes on a daily basis have unique insights into effective ways of handling those matters. Getting this type of input can help lead to productive systems and increase the ownership that those responsible for the implementation of change feel for the process.

What Will Implementation Involve?

Once a clear sense of what the problem is, how it can be solved, and who will be affected by the changes has been developed, attention to implementation will help allow for a smooth transition. Taking into consideration the organizational culture can enhance the ability of various members to perform their tasks well and contribute to higher levels of performance on other tasks. Such consideration will allow programs to be implemented in such a way as to preserve the positive aspects of current systems while enabling change that moves the organization closer to its objectives.

A clear plan should be established for phasing in changes in such a way as to allow earlier systems to be used as backup while early bugs are being worked out of new systems. Equally important, however, is a plan to finally phase out unnecessary aspects of the previous system when new ones have been firmly established to avoid redundancy. Organizational leaders should clearly communicate the process by which this transition will take place along with explanations of the impact on job responsibilities and the importance to the accomplishment of organizational goals.

Exercise 7.2

In thinking about organizations that you have been involved with, consider the following questions:

- What do information networks tell people about their role in the organization?

- How might those most adept at interacting with current systems have to change under new ones?

- What relationship exists between the handling of information and degree of power in organizations with which you have been affiliated?

- How is organizational culture linked to its hierarchical structure?

- How can change be implemented in an existing culture most smoothly?

 Review Questions

▼ How are technologies and cultures related?

▼ How do different groups in organizations perceive the nature of information and its role in organizational processes?

▼ What are some of the most basic goals of the introduction of new technologies?

▼ How do technologies impact work practices? Organizational structures?

▼ How are cultural identification and technologies related? How does identification influence resistance?

▼ In what ways does good technological innovation parallel the introduction of a new vision or cultural change processes in general?

Discussion Questions

▼ What has been your experience with technological changes? Where have people been resistant? How was that resistance treated?

▼ What was the effect of technological change on power relations? On human relations? On values?

▼ Technology implementation teams usually have strong technological expertise but lack cultural expertise, often to the demise of expensive implementations. At what points and in what ways would you involve a cultural expert? Why would this be important?

References and Recommended Readings

Groleau, C., & Taylor, J. (1996). Toward a subject-oriented worldview of information. *Canadian Journal of Communication, 21*, 243-265.

Schein, E. (1992). *Organizational culture and leadership* (2nd ed.). San Francisco: Jossey-Bass.

Zuboff, S. (1988). *In the age of the smart machine: The future of work and power.* New York: Basic Books.

Suggested Case Study

Groleau, C., & Taylor, J. (1996). Toward a subject-oriented worldview of information. *Canadian Journal of Communication, 21*, 243-265.

Managing Culture Through Transition Periods

All organizations must go through small continuous cultural adjustments to stay competitive. Occasionally, organizations encounter major transitions. Organizational transitions require managerial and leadership efforts that go beyond basic transformations in values and vision. Such transitions include the passing of a founder or long-term organizational leader; major market or economic fluctuations; mergers and acquisitions; and significant regulatory, technological, or environmental changes. As discussed throughout this book, even basic changes in organizational values can be difficult. This challenge increases substantially when management must deal with major organizational restructuring, the acquisition of an entirely different corporate culture, or the passing of a leader.

Understanding cultural change is essential to guiding a transition and assessing cultural compatibility in mergers and other restructurings. This chapter discusses the dramatic increase in these types of changes in recent years and provides an overview of instances that lead to such change. The corporate transition and integration process is nothing less than a far-reaching management change initiative for the companies or divisions involved. Just like any change initiative, managers can improve their chances of success by understanding important cultural strategies in the stages before, during, and after the transition. In this chapter, these strategies are outlined and discussed.

Key Objectives of the Chapter

▼ To aid the identification of instances that lead to dramatic organizational transitions, including the passing of a founder or leader; major market and economic changes; and organizational reorganizations such as mergers, acquisitions, strategic alliances, and divisionalization

▼ To examine how communicative activities can ease the transition between one leader and another

▼ To increase the ability to recognize types of cultural compatibility and incompatibility

▼ To investigate the ways change can be managed before, during, and after a transition

▼ To explore the methods leaders can use to create excitement, inspiration, and commitment with all people working through transition

Questions to Consider

▼ What types of market or economic fluctuations are likely to affect many companies in the next 5 years?

▼ How can organizational leaders prepare themselves and their employees for an organizational transition?

▼ What types of transitions have you experienced in organizations with which you are involved? How have organizational leaders and members reacted to such change? What strategies can leaders implement now to smooth the transition for you and other organizational members?

▶ Organizational Transition and Culture Clash

Owing to highly salient needs, organizations encountering transitions usually consider strategic, financial, and operational issues. Less thoroughly investigated are the human aspects that may lead an organization to financial failure even with the best financial plans. Far too often, personnel and culture issues are assigned a low priority during a transition period, and in other instances they are not investigated until they become a major problem. Increasing evidence suggests that cultural incompatibility is the single largest cause of failed projected performance and departure of key executives during mergers and restructurings. In terms of undergoing major cultural change, one of the riskiest times for organizations is the passage of a founder or leader.

When successfully negotiated and integrated, organizational transformations can play a major role in the growth and success of organizations. These can be invigorating periods. But although it is difficult to quantify the relative success of organizations' response to the passing of founders, statistics indicate that up to one third of mergers fail within 5 years, and as many as 80% never live up to their full expectations. Many of these failures are due to cultural, human factors, not financial or objective incompatibility. In other words, the cash flow sheets can spell wonders, but the trouble starts when organizations forget about or underanalyze the effects of dramatic change on people.

P. D. Hall and D. Norburn (1987) reviewed almost 30 major studies on the benefits and gains from mergers. They suggested two possible conclusions regarding the relation of culture (mis)match between partnering organizations and their success: (a) the extent of fit between the culture of the acquiring organization and the acquired organization is directly correlated to the success of the acquisition; and (b) here there is a lack of fit in corporate culture, the success of the acquisition is determined by the amount of postacquisition autonomy granted to the acquired organization. Clearly a need exists to understand the cultural issues involved in all transitions.

▶ The Passing of an Organizational Founder or Leader

One of the most important sources of organizational culture is the values of its founders. Even in mature companies, one can trace many organizational ideals to the beliefs of founders and early leaders. Not only do founders devise the vision in which the organization operates, they also choose the key managers who help to flesh out this mission. Founders have a major influence on how an organization initially defines its product and customers, and based on these goals, the organization develops its particular history, personality, and culture.

The Impact of Founder Values

Organizational founders usually have in common a high level of self-confidence and determination, but they typically differ in their assumptions about the nature of reality, human relationships, and the management of resources. Leader philosophies may view organizational control in manners that range from autocratic to participative, organizational decisions may be made in terms of long-term goals or short-term quotas, and product development may be seen as an integrative process or a departmental action. No matter their philosophy, however, organizational founders are similar in that they normally encourage others in the organization to take on leader values as their own.

If the visions of leaders are incorrect, the organization fails early. If their assumptions function well in the existing environment or their products are fortunate in the existing market, the company succeeds and the founder's values and practices get much credit even if chance and luck were critical elements.

Founder values are perpetuated through the organization in the form of mission statements and the prescribed vision and goals as well as through more informal organizational rituals and procedures. These values are embedded in the organizational culture through the actions of the founder and the leaders appointed by the founder, until such time as the leader must leave the organization.

The Passage of a Leader

As we enter the 21st century, many organizations are on the brink of choosing a new generation of leaders. New CEOs are present or soon anticipated at General Electric, Allied Signal, Ford, 3M, AT&T, Citicorp, and Coca-Cola, in addition to many other organizations. These organizations must find and install new leaders without impeding the momentum of the continuous transformation necessary for organizations to succeed. Some new CEOs have already had great impact. Founders and leaders pass from organizations for several reasons.

Like any mortal beings, as organizational founders grow older they will get sick and die or may wish to retire. Sometimes, successful CEOs are swayed to leave one organization to lead another. And of course, some leaders loose their jobs because they fail to effectively lead their organizations.

For organizations to flourish in the competitive work environment, strong leadership is crucial. Increasingly, organizations are focusing on founder and leader succession as one of their most important business processes. The process is complicated and political in nature, and thus organizations must proceed with care, forethought, and diligence to remain competitive during such a turbulent transformational period. How does an organization go about accomplishing such a feat?

The Transformational Framework

Several components work toward creating a successful transition from one leader to another. Noel Tichy (1996) sketches out the ideal "transformational framework." The steps in this framework all have in common the importance of strategic thinking, visioning, framing, and dialogue. In other words, forethought and planned two-way communication are essential for a smooth transition from one leader to the next.

Component 1: Identify Transformation Needs. The first component in successful leader transition is to identify the needs and goals for the transformation. This can be accomplished through external research as well as intracompany brainstorm sessions. During times of change, it may be especially worthwhile to encourage participation from multiple groups to learn more about the changes that will lead the company to success. Through off-site workshops and in-depth executive interviews, organizations can encourage employees to think creatively about the ways the organization can meet and manage the changes to come. Such pooled knowledge is essential for laying the foundation for major change.

Component 2: Develop a Mass of Leaders. Second, the organization must mobilize a critical mass of transformational leaders who will lead the company through the change. Depending on the size of the company, this group of leaders may range from five to several hundred, but they all should have several traits in common. Such leaders usually have the ability to identify changes in the environment that will affect the business, lead others in overcoming the fear and uncertainty of change, visualize business through consumers' eyes, hold a clear vision about the company's future, and take responsibility for change. As part of this effort, the organization must provide significant developmental experiences to create, nurture, and upgrade the skills of this group of transformation leaders.

Component 3: Focus on Customer Service and Financial Performance. Third, the organization should continue to focus on customer service and financial performance. As is common during any type of organizational transition, managers have the tendency to be inward looking during times of leader change. Nevertheless, during this type of change it is especially important to be aware of and responsive to one's work environment.

Component 4: Develop a New Company Vision. Fourth, the development of a new vision by all organizational leaders, including the current CEO and CEO candidates, will assist in pointing to a new beginning. Whether created by individuals or in teams, different visions can be discussed, compared, and evaluated by all candidates involved. Eventually, the new vision should be pared down and agreed on, and the CEO ultimately selected to lead the company should be committed to it. Otherwise, the organization will have to undergo another transition as it waits for an entirely new vision to develop.

Component 5: Provide a CEO Screening and Succession Process. Fifth, and last, the organization should create and provide a CEO screening and succession process. A systematic, disciplined process of screening and developing future CEOs will provide the structure needed to honestly evaluate available candidates. The best candidates should be put in key leadership positions, tested in various ways, and continuously evaluated. Found to be particularly successful in assessment is the use of 360-degree feedback, in which the individual's peers, subordinates, and boss all rate the candidate's leadership skills.

Exercise 8.1

Consider an organization in which you are currently involved or have some knowledge about—whether that be a school club, neighborhood business, or multimillion dollar company. Based on Tichy's (1996) five components for successful transformations, answer the following questions:

1. If a top leader or founder of your organization was about to quit or retire, what action steps would lead to a successful transition to another leader? Consider steps that both the departing leader, as well as other organizational leaders, should take before, during, and after the transition.

2. Do you think that your organization would actually proceed with these action steps? Why or why not? What potential organizational barriers can stand in the way of transformation plans? Are these barriers more often practical or ideological in nature?

3. Many times, organizational leader screening teams consciously or unconsciously search for new leaders who are similar to the departing leaders. What implications does this have for affirmative action and diversity programs in organizations? How can one balance the tension between hiring new leaders who possess the values and ideals of past leaders, yet also representing alternative views or backgrounds? Which is more important in what situations and why?

4. Considering the power of organizational identification and member buy-in, why do you think Tichy suggests that a fresh organizational vision accompany a new CEO? Are visions and organizational rules more powerful when employees have a voice in creating them? If so, what implications does that have in times of organizational change?

5. What are the potential advantages of a 360-degree feedback assessment instrument (as Tichy suggests for the CEO screening process)? Have you ever been involved in such an assessment, either as a recipient or as a provider of feedback? Why do you believe many organizations avoid this type of evaluation instrument?

It is possible for a change in leaders to be successful, even when a company is facing an uncertain organizational environment. With advance planning, the identification and cultivation of a critical leadership mass, and an outward focus on future goals and customer needs, the passing of a leader need not end in cultural demise. When handled with forethought, strategic visioning and two-way communication, such a transition can actually serve as a catalyst for urgently needed organizational transformation.

▶ Organizational Transition Owing to Economic, Personnel, and Market Changes

The environments in which organizations exist vary in both complexity and stability. At the one extreme is a noncomplex and stable environment in which events are predictable and placid. Companies in such environments are familiar with their surroundings and do not have to worry much about unanticipated market shifts. At the opposite extreme is a turbulent atmosphere that is dense, complicated, and quick to change. An organization with such surroundings lives in continual anticipation of environmental changes and never knows whether organizational actions may result in unanticipated consequences.

Of course, these two environments serve as symbolic poles to a continuum of different types of organizational situations. Near the placid, calm pole, one would find, for instance, a public utility company, a monopoly with a developed line of work and consistent supply and demand. Of increasing interest, however, are the growing number of companies that are grouped on the turbulent end of the pole. These types of companies have complex environments and unstable, quickly changing products. For example, computer software businesses must constantly research and anticipate the latest changes in technology, governmental regulations, and competitor products. Below we review several of the main reasons why organizations increasingly have to deal with major economic or market changes.

Deregulation

In the past 20 years, many industries that had comfortably survived in monopolistic industries for years suddenly had to face an environment of deregulation. For example, such companies have to change from values based on entitlement to those based on customer needs. Since the

Bell telephone monopoly was dismantled in 1984, all telecommunications companies have had to radically change their way of viewing the product and customers. For the first time, companies such as AT&T had to fundamentally change organizational culture to keep up with the competition.

Downsizing

According to Tom Peters (1987) and as discussed by Eric Eisenberg and H. L. Goodall (1993), some U.S. companies are unresponsive to environmental information because of a bias in favor of giantism, or the belief that bigger is better. To be competitive in ever more complex environments, however, organizations are learning that they must be hierarchically flatter. Thus, information can be quickly shared throughout different hierarchical levels and organizations can be oriented toward niche markets. Organizations have had to undergo major organizational changes, often including corporate downsizing, to stay flexible and oriented toward customer needs and competitive pressures. A Towers-Perrin consulting firm survey in late 1995 found that two thirds of white-collar employees reported that their companies had downsized or undergone major restructuring during the previous 2 years (cited in Conrad & Poole, 1998, p. 20). This change in corporate structure often dictates a parallel alteration of corporate culture.

Technological Innovation

As discussed in Chapter 7, the introduction of technology can bring about major changes that require fundamental cultural transitions. For instance, the massive introduction of the personal computer (PC) has constituted a major environmental jolt to computer hardware and software companies. Although the PC has fueled and instigated work in smaller companies such as Microsoft and Apple, it initially affected the computer giant IBM in a negative manner. Used to long-term projects, large corporate accounts, and a virtual monopoly, IBM was forced to completely reanalyze its corporate culture to adapt to changing consumer needs and ever-increasing competition from smaller, more flexible companies.

With the introduction of new technologies, companies are wise to consider both positive and negative results. For instance, although the introduction of email may assist an organization in networking between several of its regional plants, it may also encourage excessive socializing and joking that is ultimately nonproductive. In fact, many companies have been forced to backpedal when they learn that a new technology, such as the use of the Internet, has caused more harm than good. As with all change efforts, organizations must incorporate cultural considerations when introducing new office technologies.

Globalization

As Eisenberg and Goodall (1993) discuss, business is increasingly moving to a global marketplace. Over 100,000 U.S. companies do business abroad, and about a third of the profits of U.S. companies as well as one sixth of the nation's jobs come from international business. For instance, half of Xerox's 110,000 employees work overseas; half of Sony's employees are not Japanese. This trend in globalization impacts the way companies do business. Many companies have shut down U.S. industrial centers to relocate in areas with cheaper labor and materials. For instance, the Nike shoe company employs no Americans to manufacture shoes. The company's shoe manufacturing plants are located in Third World countries such as Indonesia, where they pay employees as little as 40 cents a day. Differences in trade policies, labor costs, and national culture can result in ethical dilemmas and international misunderstandings. These types of transitions require major changes in organizational culture.

Changing Types of Work

In the last half of the 20th century, businesspeople have seen a dramatic shift away from tangible resources toward less tangible, largely symbolic resources. Over 50% of the U.S. labor force is currently involved in the gathering, entering, formatting, and transmittal of information, and this percentage rises to more than 80% in the service industry. In addition, the number of workers who hold power because of their specialized knowledge is increasing substantially. Under the "knowledge worker" umbrella stand research scientists, teachers, and financial analysts. Although knowledge work products are more intangible, they are crucial in today's society. Among the many cultural shifts that organizations must make to accommodate this new base of workers is the continual (re)education required to update workers with the latest skills and expertise.

Knowledge and power by themselves, however, are not enough to be successful in today's organization. Relationships, forged both in and between organizations, are increasingly important. Informal relationships allow employees to get things done across functions within organizations. Some believe that the growing relational basis of power has unfavorable implications for women and minorities. Nevertheless, informal networks will no doubt be important in defining organizational cultures of tomorrow. Indeed, as we enter the 21st century, those who hold such relationships, along with those who have access to the most current information or specialized knowledge, are most likely to hold power in organizations. To succeed, organizations must adapt their culture and values to accommodate this shifting power base.

Exercise 8.2

Imagine that you are an executive manager of a relatively small company (around 100 employees) that is developing software for an online investment corporation.

- How could the preceding changes impact your organization? As a manager, how could you prepare and manage such changes?

- Must change always be difficult? How can managers frame turbulence and change as an opportunity rather than as a problem?

- Within the next 10 years, which of the preceding conditions do you believe will still be important issues? Which issues do you think will begin to be less significant?

- What other issues, not listed above, do you believe will become important for organizational transformation in the future (e.g., the transformation of organizations to Internet-based businesses)?

▶ Mergers, Acquisitions, and Other Corporate Reorganizations

In recent years, mergers, acquisitions, and other corporate reorganizations have dominated the business landscape. Beyond the melodramatic excitement that characterizes these transitions, there is a human side to these reorganizations, with the lives of millions of employees affected by one decision. In the United States alone, more than 25% of the workforce has been affected by major reorganization activity during the 1990s, meaning that somehow they were touched by a corporate merger, acquisition (or takeover), divisionalization, or formal strategic alliance.

Types of Reorganization Transitions

Reorganizations have long been considered the exclusive work of economists, market strategists, and financial advisors, but organizational leaders are learning that the personnel factor is equally important in determining the success or failure in a reorganization. Depending on the reasons for change, organizational leaders should consider several factors.

Mergers and Acquisitions. In the past 10 years, there have been over 23,000 registered acquisitions in the United States. Why this boom in merger and acquisition (M&A) activity? The following factors can be considered to have facilitated the current wave of reorganization activity. First, M&A activity provides a convenient means of "going global" as well as eliminating competition. Second, in the 1980s, organizations increased their borrowing capacity, and the surplus of capital was used in large part to acquire new companies. Third, an increasing number of companies have come to the market for sale. Last, and most important, has been the easing of government regulations.

M&A activity is usually considered to be rational, financial, and in the best interests of the organization's shareholders. Because financial and strategic factors dominate M&A selection reasons, the human factor is sometimes ignored. Nevertheless, issues of culture and culture clash quickly appear when two or more companies come together as one. Although M&As may indeed fail for financial and economic reasons, one of the main reasons for failure lies in culture clash.

Divisionalization. Although giantism through mergers and acquisitions has the advantages of financial stability and reduced competition, many experts argue that there is no effective way to manage a company with more than 10,000 employees. As discussed, corporate leaders have come to realize that bigger does not always mean better, and some have outsourced and downsized to flatten the hierarchy of their organization.

Another way that organizations have dealt with giantism is to "divisionalize," in the sense of decentralizing functions into autonomous product or market units. This is true in the case of General Motors, a company that has opted to introduce a special class of automobiles through the separate company of Saturn. As divisions develop their own history, they begin to develop a separate culture as well.

Strong divisional subcultures can become problematic when the larger organization decides to impose company-wide rules that may not be compatible with other parts of the organization. Some companies avoid this problem by not imposing company-wide policies, but many of the most successful multidivisional corporations—such as IBM and General Motors—do preserve a strong company-wide organizational culture. Managers should weigh the costs and benefits of managing individual subcultures before making a move to divisionalization.

Strategic Alliances and Joint Ventures. Corporate strategic alliances and joint ventures have become increasingly popular as organizations have hoped to draw on each other's strengths when breaking into new products and markets. In fact, many public relations and marketing companies are beginning to offer facilitation of such alliances as part of their publicity package of organizational services. When corporations form strategic alliances, they do not attempt to completely meld together disparate cultures. Cultural compatibility and trust in the partnering organization(s), however, are integral to making the joint alliance successful. Found to be especially important in determining the success of such ventures are the company policies and managerial styles of leaders working on the joint venture.

Issues in Forging Cultural Relations

All changes that bring cultures into contact require the use of the cultural change processes detailed in earlier chapters. The degree of cultural compatibility and the end relation desired dictate what is to be accomplished in that change process.

Cultural Compatibility. Cultural compatibility may seem outwardly equivalent to cultural similarity. Although this notion makes common sense, empirical evidence does not prove that culture similarity equals reorganization success. Perhaps more worthwhile is analysis of *what constitutes* the current cultures of partnering organizations and *how* the organizations will meld together. In regard to the first question, a number of contrasting styles in organizations exist that can create a problem when the organizations combine. In the first chapter these were described as the character of cultures.

When merging organizations hold some of the same goals and philosophies, there is a higher likelihood of success, and thus it is easiest to find strategic and cultural fits within specific industries. For instance, Nabisco and Standard Brands were a compatible fit because of complementary products and distribution. Before merging, not only did the corporate leaders of the two organizations talk about assets and cash flow, but they also discussed similar customers, business philosophies, and plans for future work.

On the other hand, cross-industry combinations often yield conflicting cultures. Mobil's management of Montgomery Ward is a representative example. Whereas Mobile holds a long-term mind-set typical to exploration companies, Montgomery Ward is focused on a short-term retailing perspective.

The Cultural Relation Desired. The issue of cultural compatibility thus has much to do with the merging companies' philosophies and goals. Just as important, however, is the issue of the *type* of organizational partnership agreement desired. Depending on the motives, objectives, and power dynamics of the combination, this partnership agreement—or "marriage contract"—can take one of three different forms, according to Sue Cartwright and Cary L. Cooper (1992): the open marriage, the traditional marriage, or the modern or collaborative marriage.

Autonomy or Semiautonomy in Open Marriages. The basis of the "open marriage" is a policy of noninterference. The acquiring organization graciously allows the acquired organization to function in a fairly autonomous manner. The goal of this hands-off approach is to create mutual support and synergy without necessarily changing the original natures of the combining organizations.

The open marriage approach is appropriate when the acquisition or the acquired company promises future growth and already has in place a competent management team. Although semiautonomy often works well for both related and unrelated acquisitions, many acquirers seem unable to resist the temptation to change things, just because they can. Nevertheless, the old adage, "If it ain't broke, don't fix it," is often the best advice. A clear tolerance for multiculturalism can be the first step to ensuring a successful corporate combination.

Open marriages can falter when financial results decline or the acquired organization's management becomes weak. In these cases it is likely that the acquirer will lose trust in the union and resort to a more controlling type of organizational marriage.

Absorbing or Assimilating in Traditional Marriage. When the acquiring partner is dissatisfied with or does not agree with the present performance or philosophies of the acquired organization, assimilation will likely occur. This is analogous to a traditional marriage in which the dominant partner imposes all of its goals and beliefs on the smaller, less powerful partner. In this type of union, the acquirer attempts to redesign the acquired organization so that it fits its own goals and values.

For traditional marriages to be successful, the dominant partner must be sensitive to and prepare for resistance, while the acquired partner must be amenable to change. The acquirer should design a detailed plan on how to acculturate acquired employees to new practices, procedures, and philosophies. Traditional marriages run into problems when the acquired group resists the culture of the dominant group. Based on the way most M&As are currently managed, we would say that most corporate reorganizations fall into the traditional marriage type.

Co-Creating and Collaborating in Modern Marriage. Possibly the most progressive, but most difficult, type of merger is the collaborative, "modern marriage." This type of union can only occur when organizational leaders from the partnering organizations commit themselves to extensive communication and are able to recognize and appreciate each other's strengths and weaknesses. In contrast to the other two types of marriages, where the old culture of both or one of the companies is preserved, in the modern marriage the two organizations combine to form a new vision together.

For a collaborative union to work, with a new culture based on the "best of both worlds," both organizations must be open to share ideas. For all their strengths, collaborative marriages can develop difficulties. For instance, because they are so rare, employees often react as if they were experiencing a traditional type of marriage, with one group of employees feeling that they are taking over (or have been taken over) by the other. To avoid this problem, managers must clearly communicate the goals of the union and act promptly to diffuse any feelings of threat between the two merging groups. In addition, because this type of collaboration takes extensive time and effort, it can be more costly than the other two types of unions.

Communicative Strategies for the Successful Merging of Cultures

For mergers and acquisitions to be successful, members on both sides must understand, recognize, and accept the type of partnership they are embarking on. In acquisitions, the power dynamics are quite clear-cut and acquired employees are likely to realize that they have little choice but to adapt to the new culture. In mergers, however, power dynamics are more ambiguous, and the terms of the partnership must be clearly negotiated and communicated.

The development and implementation of a specific plan of action before, during, and after the merger or acquisition can greatly increase chances for organizational marriage success. The following guide for organizations going through the M&A process is developed from the works of Richard Bibler (1989) and Sue Cartwright and Cary Cooper (1992). The courtship and marriage metaphor is continued here.

Precombination—"Courtship"

1. Know thyself. Before an organization should even consider merging with another, it should take stock of its own corporate philosophies, goals, and visions. This is more difficult than it first might seem. Without careful consideration, it is easy to view one's own quirks—whether an autocratic supervisory structure or a set of participatory socialization rituals—as normal, natural, or intrinsically right. Through the recogni-

tion of corporate strengths and weaknesses, however, managers are made aware of the unique qualities their own organization possesses and the qualities to look for in a partner. In addition, by better knowing themselves potential partners can more clearly articulate and evaluate culture traits.

2. Know thy partner. Before embarking on an organizational partnership, organization leaders should be aware of the strengths, weaknesses, and quirks of the potential partner. Although managers traditionally do a good job of evaluating a potential partner's financial and product information, it is easy to forget about the human aspects of the organization. Nevertheless, managers increase their chances of success by developing a profile of the potential partner's culture and comparing it to their own. Components to this profile include compensation packages, performance appraisal systems, hiring and firing criteria, and the philosophies of dominant leaders (especially if leaders from both organizations are going to stay on).

3. Clarify the partnership agreement. After the two organizations feel they know themselves and are compatible with each other, it is important to have a clearly articulated merger contract. If the terms of the union are incorrectly understood by either of the partners—say, one party believes it is entering a collaborative marriage, whereas the other expects a traditional one—anguish and financial demise are likely to occur.

Formal Organizational Combination—
"The Marriage Announcement and Honeymoon"

1. Implement an announcement plan. Shocking information is usually better communicated face to face than in a written manner. The announcement time should be synchronized to avoid distortion and exaggeration of the information. The messenger is also an important part of the announcement. Research indicates that employees best receive news of change informally from people they know and trust—such as from their direct supervisors. Therefore, news of change might best be communicated in a one-to-one or small group environment, a format that is personal and allows for employee feedback. To acquired employees, the person(s) communicating change—whether a direct supervisor, acquisition manager, or evaluating team—become the "face" of the acquiring

organization. This person or team of people should hold strong leadership qualities, be familiar with both the acquiring and acquired organization, and be prepared to effectively manage employee resistance.

2. Allow for feedback and organizational grief. After employees hear about the organizational combination, they likely will have questions and concerns. Managers can provide opportunities for immediate feedback through question-and-answer forums and for continual feedback through programs such as email discussion groups and interorganizational team-building forums. By encouraging employee feedback, managers can reassure others that they have no "hidden agendas." In addition, managers should expect and allow for a period of organizational grief. Many people are uncomfortable with change, especially when they feel they have no control over it. Managers should avoid telling employees that they must adapt immediately. Employees are likely to respond more positively if they feel they have time to adapt and have some voice in the change.

3. Be open about potential culture changes. It is difficult for employees to determine how or if they want to fit into a new culture if they do not know much about it. Managers should be clear on the type of organizational marriage (open, traditional, collaborative) employees should expect. This includes referring to areas where people will have to make clear culture changes. By maintaining high visibility and honest communication, managers can reduce employee fear and resistance to new ideas. Not surprising, what people object to more than change is the feeling that they are being lied to, rebuffed, or ignored.

4. Prepare for and prevent voluntary staff turnover. Mergers and acquisitions are associated with high levels of staff turnover. In fact, several studies report a managerial quitting rate as high as 75%. Some organizational managers appear to believe this rate of turnover is inevitable, uncontrollable, and sometimes even desirable. Nevertheless, this attitude toward human capital has many shortcomings, and turnover can be reduced when managers plan for the prevention of it. For instance, acquirers can stage welcoming or integrative ceremonies for the acquired organization. Culture change can also be facilitated through changes in the physical environment of the workplace. Last, people usually appraise change as either posing a threat or an opportunity. Through different

framing devices (see Chapter 4), managers can do much to promote the corporate reorganization as creating new opportunities for those involved.

Postcombination—Making the Marriage Work

1. Keep up the effort. No matter how good the precombination plan and the merger announcement system, the postcombination phase can be problematic if managers do not continue communication efforts. Change is considered to be a three-stage process comprising (a) the unfreezing of existing attitudes, (b) the introduction of change, and (c) the refreezing of new attitudes and the development of new group norms. A corporate reorganization faces continuous challenges and leaders must be flexible in the way they continually agree on and communicate organizational values, goals, and philosophies.

2. Develop a new vision and mission that are continually reinforced through framing. After the merger announcement, managers from both organizations should come together and develop a new corporate vision. Even in traditional marriages, where one organization's views will prevail over those of the other, the action of co-creating a new vision has several benefits. First, it clearly articulates organization goals. Second, a co-created vision will likely motivate buy-in from the acquired organization. Third, a vision statement serves as a management guide to track everyday framing actions and behaviors. Of course, some employees may resist the new vision, especially if they feel their beliefs and values are not represented in it. Nevertheless, the creation of a vision statement often provides a much-needed opportunity for resentments to be aired and dealt with.

3. Create and communicate a new personnel plan fast. Merger integration has sometimes been compared to pulling off a Band-Aid: It can be slow and painful or fast and painful. One of the largest areas for confusion after a merger is related to organizational structure and compensation changes. The sooner that changes can be finalized and implemented, even if they include downsizing or geographic relocations, the sooner ambiguity and gossip can be terminated. One of the most sensitive issues is compensation. People understand compensation to

equal worth, value, and status. Through prompt evaluations and modifications in pay and benefits packages, organizations can help to prevent resistance and resentment that can result from compensation differentials.

4. Deal with employee stress. Change is potentially stressful for all concerned. Those who have initiated a merger or acquisition have a stake in seeing it succeed, whereas those in the acquired organization may feel out of control. Meanwhile, middle managers are often put into the role of messenger—having to communicate the mandates of top managers to unsuspecting and resistant workers. Middle managers also face the dilemma of being too young to qualify for voluntary retirement but too old to find a better job. Research findings have shown that it is more the expectancy of change and fears of the future that cause stress than the actual change process itself. Therefore, as previously discussed, communication and overcommunication are extremely important to lessen stress levels in the workplace. Managers can also address the problem by providing stress counselors and stress management training programs and using attitude surveys. The participation, and thus endorsement, of senior managers in such intervention programs has been found to greatly increase their organizational acceptance and success.

5. Monitor success and continue to keep in touch. Once integration is begun, the main goal of communication is to supplement initial information and give direction so that values and beliefs can be reflected in behavioral practices. Dealing with the human factor of corporate reorganizations is a reasonably long-term and time-consuming project. It is therefore desirable from the outset to identify a specific person or team of people to be responsible for merger communication, while at the same time making use of existing communication networks that are familiar and comfortable. Feedback and open information mechanisms introduced in the early stages should remain in place long after the original combination to avoid the resurrection of fears and insecurities.

6. Recognize the warning signs of culture dysfunction. To proactively manage the human side of mergers and acquisitions, managers must be wary of signs that cultural integration has gone awry. Warning signs can take on a number of different faces, but managers should

be particularly concerned if they suddenly see lowered productivity coupled with high rates of turnover and absenteeism. Other indicators include a rising incidence of customer complaints, low level of employee participation in meetings or social events, and an increased frequency in short-term medical absences (possibly to attend job interviews or because employees are experiencing job-related stress and sickness).

By using the communicative tools provided in this chapter, managers can dramatically increase the probability of merger and acquisition success. Employees will be better informed and know how to react to the new organization. This is not to say that any of the organizational transitions described in this chapter are easy to deal with. Admittedly, these types of transitions—the passage of a founder, major economic or market turbulence, and corporate reorganization—are three of the most complex culture challenges for organizations. Nevertheless, through open communication and advance planning managers can provide an atmosphere of trust and community. This, in turn, will result in less employee stress, fewer employee defections, and increased productivity and profitability.

Exercise 8.3

Imagine you are the acquisition manager of ABC, Inc. Your company is merging with a smaller company, called ZZZ. Throughout the next week, ZZZ employees will be moving into the ABC place of business.

* Based on the preceding discussion, what types of organizational processes and personnel activities will you institute or conduct during this first week to ease the transition?

* What are both advantages and potential downsides to these processes and activities?

* What might be the positive and negative reactions of employees in both companies?

▶ **Discussion Questions**

Mark Sirower described the "failed" AT&T acquisition of NCR in 1991 as follows:

> It is a mystery why, after losing an estimated $2 billion in its own com-
> puter business between 1985 and 1990, AT&T's directors were willing to
> approve the payment of a 4.2 billion premium for the NCR acquisition—a
> 125% premium above the pre-bid share price of the company. Charles
> Exley, chairman and CEO for NCR at the time, accused AT&T of merely
> trying to bail out its own failed strategy for marketing computers.
>
> He may have been right on target. After paying the extraordinary
> premium for NCR, AT&T voluntarily left NCR executives in place to
> conduct business as usual for two years after the acquisition. In fact they
> were even put in charge of AT&T's old computer production and mar-
> keting business. NCR executives were merely asked by AT&T to "look"
> for synergy. The vision was that there would be "convergence" between
> computers and communications, but AT&T technological advantage was
> in telecom switches, not in the corporate or consumer computer business.
>
> By 1993, when earnings began to decline, AT&T signaled somewhat
> belatedly that it had a strategy for NCR after all. It appointed its own
> executive, Jerre Stead, to run the computer division, but synergies did
> not materialize. In fact, between 1993 and 1995 most of NCR's top man-
> agers left the company. Costs increased dramatically as hundreds of new
> sales teams in over 100 countries were set up and the company was
> pushed into new markets and industries where it had little experience.
> The result was that AT&T shareholders lost the entire premium and
> racked up losses of $270 million in 1995 alone. (pp. 34-35)

▼ What are some of the mistakes AT&T made based on your understanding of initiating cultural change?

▼ What kind of marriage did AT&T have in mind? Why did that not ma-
terialize?

▼ What preparation could AT&T have made to create the possibility of greater synergy?

▼ What do you know about the prevailing cultures at AT&T an NCR at that time?

▼ What were likely cultural clashes?

▼ What can be learned from Tichy's (1996) "ideal transformation framework" that might be applied to AT&T's failures or current attempts with a new CEO to change its place in the telecommunication industry?

▶ Review Questions

▼ Why are transitions becoming increasingly important as we head toward the 21st century?

▼ What types of transitions do managers have control over? How can organizational leaders approach these transitions differently from ones that are less under management control?

▼ How is the passing of a founder best managed?

▼ What are the advantages and disadvantages of mergers and acquisitions? What cultural factors must leaders take into account when factoring such cost/benefit analyses?

▼ Is one type of organizational marriage intrinsically better than another? If so, why or when?

▼ Is there a difference between framing reorganizations in the best light and brainwashing employees? What ethical dilemmas must managers grapple with before, during, and after a corporate reorganization?

▶ References and Recommended Readings

Bibler, R. (1989). *The Arthur Young management guide to mergers and acquisitions.* New York: John Wiley.

Cartwright, S., & Cooper, C. (1992). *Mergers and acquisitions: The human factor.* Oxford, UK: Butterworth Heinemann.

Conrad, C., & Poole, M. S. (1998). *Strategic organizational communication: Into the twenty-first century* (4th ed.). Fort Worth, TX: Harcourt Brace College Publishers.

Eisenberg, E., & Goodall, H. L., Jr. (1993). *Organizational communication: Balancing creativity and constraint.* New York: St. Martin's Press.

Hall, P. D., & Norburn, D. (1987). The management factor in acquisition performance. *Leadership and Organizational Development Journal, 8,* 23-30.

Peters, T. (1987). *Thriving on chaos.* New York: Alfred A. Knopf.

Schein, E. (1992). *Organizational culture and leadership* (2nd ed.). San Francisco: Jossey-Bass.

Sirower, M. (1997). *The synergy trap: How companies lose the acquisition game.* New York: Free Press.

Tichy, N. (1996, Spring). Simultaneous transformation and CEO succession: Key to global competitiveness. *Organizational Dynamics,* pp. 45-59.

9

Managing Culture in Multinational Organizations

Overview

The difficulty in managing internal cultural differences is compounded when organizations span national boundaries. Since the nature of international business partnerships varies widely today, an organization must be adaptive to each unique set of circumstances.

Despite the uniqueness of situations, several common pitfalls face the transnational organization today. This chapter explores the complexities of managing hearts, minds, and souls across national boundaries. A central issue is the complex tensions that exist between integration and healthy diversity as well as between adaptation and change processes. Cultural sensitivity and skills in intercultural communication are discussed.

Organizations often face difficulties when they use expatriate employees in sites abroad. Typically, organizations that operate on a global level use some combination of employees from the local site and from the parent company. Although this can be extremely beneficial at times, it can also lead to complications if certain factors are not accounted for. A careful consideration of how people must negotiate cultural differences can aid transnational companies—and nicely illustrate other sets of cultural issues.

Key Objectives of the Chapter

▼ To aid identification of common pitfalls faced by transnational organizations in managing culture

▼ To increase sensitivity to how cultural differences may influence success or failure of an international venture

▼ To increase understanding of programs or training that address cultural differences in organizations

▼ To aid identification of strength and weakness in an organization's orientation to cultural difference

▼ To aid in the development of plans improving an organization's sensitivity to cross-cultural needs

▼ To increase understanding of key predictors of success and failure in international business

Questions to Consider

▼ Consider an organization with a clear international presence, ideally one in which you have some involvement. Or if you are at a university, consider the relation of the university to students from other countries and national subcultures.

▼ If you were a decision-making member, what could you do to increase the development of systems responsive to cultural difference?

▼ What are the core cultural beliefs of the parent organization?

▼ What cultural beliefs are manifest by cross-cultural subsidiaries or affiliates?

▼ In what areas might these cultures encounter conflict?

▼ How might fundamental differences be negotiated to help move the organization toward fulfillment of its goals?

▼ Are the fundamental goals of subsidiary sections at odds with one another?

▼ What are the types of recurrent conflicts or problems encountered by this organization in its international endeavors?

▶ The Transnational Organization Today

Increasing numbers of large U.S. corporations today have sites in multiple countries. Usually, such expansions of the parent company are initially undertaken to increase the cost-effectiveness of production practices at home. At times, the motivation is procurement of natural resources, at others, the availability of labor. Once they are established abroad, however, it is not uncommon for these companies to examine ways to tap local markets and expand distribution of product lines or services. The driving force behind such undertakings tends to be the achievement of global competitiveness.

Managing a global operation is far from a simple process, as goals, motivations, and desired outcomes may vary widely by geographic location. Increasingly, managers are aware that developing workplaces that are sensitive and responsive to the array of cultural differences exhibited across various sites is crucial to success in the global marketplace.

A Whole New Set of Cultural Complexities

Examinations of cultural differences in organizational subgroups and between merging organizations has already demonstrated the many ways in which cultural conflict can hinder productivity and lead to demoralization. All of these factors have relevance in multinational organizations as well, but these organizations also include another dimension of cultural complexity. When dealing with organizations that span national boundaries, attention must be lent to the differences in national cultures of the parent company and its subsidiaries abroad. Differences between the two complicate the achievement of organizational goals and potentially lead to increased employee turnover or other destabilizing effects in branch locations.

Identifying Sources of Difficulty

An organization's relationship to the international market is influenced by many factors. Some corporations have branch offices aimed at providing similar products and services to different markets. Others have site locations where functions performed vary greatly from one locale to the next. Large conglomerates may own companies in many locations, each providing goods for a particular niche market, whereas in other circumstances alliances between two organizations from different parent countries may create distinct organizational sites that must be responsive to the direction of two different entities.

To increase managers' awareness about potential areas of difficulty, the relationship between a given organization and its subsidiaries or affiliates abroad must be identified. In doing so, the goals and desired outcomes of each entity should be examined. What are the priorities of each of the branch sites? Are any of those goals in conflict with one another? Do the core values of geographically disbursed sites stand in conflict with one another in any way?

Answering these questions can help identify areas in which the potential for system breakdown is high. Imposing the cultural norms and expectations of the parent company on a branch location is likely to create conflict and reduce effective communication among organizational members. On the other hand, allowing a branch site complete autonomy can create dilemmas of its own. Often, the ultimate responsibility for product and service outcome lies with the parent company.

For this reason, among others, it is important to find a way to negotiate a space in which the national values and cultural norms of the host country are accounted for and integrated in work practices. Still, the mission and goals of the parent organization should not be lost or corrupted.

Preparing Expatriated Employees for Success

A common difficulty faced by multinational organizations is that of placing organizational members who are not native to the host country in sites located abroad. Although most organizations see such placements as important for business, they can become problematic. Expatriates often have trouble adjusting to the host culture at both the national and organizational levels.

Expectations of work performance and authority vary considerably from one locale to another, and being ill prepared to negotiate those differences can create both personal and professional hardship for employees. In addition, such work experiences place burdens on the families of those assigned to live abroad. Frank discussion of such factors with organizational members initially can help reduce the likelihood of employees leaving for personal reasons down the road.

To avoid common pitfalls when placing employees in overseas locations, managers should take certain preparatory and preventive measures before employees leave their native country. Any organization that routinely engages in expatriate placement should have systems in place to help prepare its employees for work abroad. Training employees to be sensitive to cultural differences and adequately preparing them for the different expectations that may be placed on them can help ease the culture shock that is traditionally experienced.

Choosing to place employees who demonstrate a high degree of intercultural skill is also helpful. This goes far beyond proficiency in foreign language. Interculturally adept individuals are responsive to varied perspectives and willing to seek out and develop a greater understanding of the cultural expectations at different sites.

For this to be effective, however, attention must be given to the relationship between the parent organization and its affiliates from their inception. Cultural sensitivity is important for members across the organization, and concerted effort to develop trust across cultural boundaries will lay a more solid foundation for organizational excellence. Particularly in situations where appointments are in flux, clearly defined roles will allow employees to move in and out of them more comfortably and provide more stability for the organization. Along the same lines, clear sources of support and proactive efforts on the organization's part to help integrate expatriates into organizational life will allow a more comfortable fit to develop.

The Role of Communication

As with other instances of cultural management, here again, the role of clearly communicated objectives from management is vital. Since it is not only language that varies from culture to culture but also forms of appropriate speech, leadership must be acutely aware of these factors when framing messages across organizational sites. What is and is not appropriately discussed in different settings varies widely. It is important to keep in mind that the fundamental goal one seeks to achieve is not necessarily a function of the message that would be used to convey that desire in one's native country.

A focus not on the message but on the ultimate goal that one seeks to achieve can allow for a different perspective. By taking this approach, one can more easily evaluate whether or not that goal is in keeping with the values and norms of the host culture. If it is not, then an assessment of the necessity of accomplishing that particular goal might be helpful or its site of implementation might need to be reconsidered. If it is in keeping with the culture of the target site, managers should find culturally sensitive and appropriate means of communicating that goal.

Management groups can also actively work to create opportunities for expatriates to contribute to operations and feel rewarded for their contributions. As with any organizational site, increased identification with the affiliate site will generally lead to greater employee satisfaction and increased productivity. In a situation where the organizational member is already less identified with the host culture, identification with the organizational site is especially important both for the employee personally and for his or her ability and desire to contribute significantly to the development of the organization.

Although it may be attractive to a parent organization to place exemplary employees from home in a site abroad because of their commitment to organizational ideals, this can sometimes lead to problems in communication on the other end. The entrenched cultural position of dominant managerial groups can make flexibility and adaptiveness difficult. It is possible for what makes an individual most successful in one locale to be precisely the thing that impedes his or her performance elsewhere. Careful assessment of individuals' ability to negotiate cultural differences ought to be considered prior to placing them in a different cultural milieu.

Balancing Cultural Adaptiveness and Encouraging Good Business

In many circumstances a parent corporation has ethical obligations to retain certain degrees of control over the practices of affiliate sites. Similarly, sound economic sense may require similar practices in different sites. Needs of organizational control, cultural management, and cultural conflict usually arise together. The organization must have a clear and unwavering vision and mission that it seeks to accomplish. Only in doing so can it provide a framework in which individual cultures can work toward achievement of the same goal.

Similarly, systems of participation take on new significance in organizations that overtly have a broad range of different perspectives and needs to address. Creating systems that are responsive to the different cultural needs of employees at different sites but also actively considering the interests of the communities in which those sites are located is important. In such systems, conflict can arise productively to stimulate innovation and growth rather than serving as a catalyst for entrenchment or decay.

Exercise 9.1

- What are several ethical considerations of going multinational?

- How would you consider potential impacts that a company would have on the local value system?

- Is it possible to separate human rights issues from cultural differences? If a certain pay scale or working condition is considered unethical in your home country, should it automatically be considered unethical in an affiliate country? Why or why not? What circumstances would you consider in making this decision?

- How would you define cultural imperialism? What forms of cultural imperialism (if any) are appropriate when going transnational?

- What are potential costs for not imposing home company values and norms on an affiliate company?

▶ Gauging Cultural Adaptivity

Several factors should be considered as an organization considers opening branches abroad or attempts to assess the effectiveness of their current systems. The following discussion examines steps ideally taken prior to the creation of an international venture. The points, however, can as easily be used to assess systems already in existence.

Cultural Assessment

Before beginning an international undertaking, whether opening a new site or embarking on a joint venture, a careful cultural analysis should be conducted. This involves examining the multiple cultural dimensions in the parent organization and developing a clear understanding of the national culture in which the parent company is embedded. After such an understanding is developed, a similar assessment of the culture of the target location or venture associates must be conducted. As this process is undertaken, careful examination of work roles and expectations, motivating forces, and standard employment practices can provide insight into the ways in which people's orientation to work and to the broader organizational mission may differ between sites.

Identifying Areas of Commonality and Difference

Following a clear articulation of the cultural components of each of these entities, identifying places in which the cultures may be highly compatible can provide insight into useful ways of approaching business. Shared values or common beliefs can be built on to move the cocultural organization toward fulfillment of its mission. At the same time, identifying areas of divergence and incompatibility can allow for insight into areas where forms of cultural training and accommodation practices will be important to success.

Complexities are encountered when cultural expectations of work roles and job performance diverge. Subtle differences may at times be more difficult to negotiate than more overt ones, as those encountering conflict may have little more than a sense of unease, discomfort, and dissatisfaction. As these lead to decreasing levels of productivity or distract from job performance, leadership may have a hard time identifying the source of the problem if careful cultural assessments have not been conducted beforehand.

Having Clearly Shared Goals

Just as it is important for an organization to have a clearly articulated vision or mission that is shared internally, international endeavors must be guided and structured in the same way. When opening a site abroad or developing a partnership with an international organization, having a clearly articulated sense of where the newly created entity is headed is important. With the first two steps completed, the articulation of such goals can allow one to compare the espoused goals with the cultural norms and motivations in use on all sides.

Only when areas of incompatibility are identified can they be addressed. In international business, negotiating shared values is a key to success, and negotiation generally is possible if a clear sense of where the various entities are starting from is established at the outset. As this step is undertaken, the rationale for an international affiliation should be articulated clearly. What purpose does establishing this entity overseas serve? Who stands to gain most from this endeavor? Building an awareness of the driving force behind the project gives the venture a firm sense of direction as it gets under way.

Developing Plans for Autonomy

Although it is almost always necessary for the parent company to have significant oversight early on in the development process, as an international venture gets under way, clearly establishing mechanisms for autonomous operations will be important to the sustained success of the entity abroad. For affiliate employees at that site to develop a sense of identification with and affinity for the organizational site, there must be a sense that what is accomplished there is important in its own right.

At the same time, for effective decisions to be made in a timely fashion, mechanisms for making them in ways that reflect cultural norms and that can be adopted and subscribed to by organizational members must be developed. For efficiency to be maximized, however, it is important that the organizational plan and goals described above be clearly articulated. In this way, the joint goal of the parent organization and its international affiliate can be used as a guiding mechanism to help frame and structure a decision-making process that the parent entity need not be involved in directly on a day-to-day basis.

Determining Optimum Structure

Another key decision in the creation of an international site is the careful structuring of its organizational systems. Clearly, deciding who will be responsible for management and what decisions these persons will have authority over is essential to smooth operation. Particularly in a situation where cultural expectations of systems of authority and control differ widely, carefully considering the response to and effectiveness of varied structural possibilities can lead the organization toward culturally sensitive and effective operations more swiftly.

Further at issue is the degree of decision-making authority to be held among key stakeholders. The parent corporation will generally want to retain authority to make some decisions. If the overseas operation is the result of a joint venture with another organization, determining the degree of control each of those entities will have is important to establish early on to avoid potential confusion and conflict as the organization evolves. Similarly, the autonomous decision-making system already developed for the affiliate organization must be respected.

Obviously, the potential for conflict and problems is quite high when multiple entities based in different geographical locations and sharing different cultural norms and value systems have authority over the operations of a particular site. Although some conflict is healthy for organizational growth, clear structural guidelines and agreements can help reduce unproductive conflict as well as allow those groups best suited to particular tasks to perform them unimpeded.

Formalizing Organizational Structure

After it is clearly established which entities are to be responsible for the management and oversight of which systems, it is important that such agreements be formalized. Creating an agreement between the interested parties that articulates this system both reduces potential conflict down the road, and provides opportunity for those involved to discuss and understand the rationale behind the systems agreement and how its structure helps fulfill the greater goals and mission previously established.

Employee Placement and Workforce Development

After an organizational goal is established and a structural design is developed to implement and oversee it, the selection of employees to carry it out can lead to the success or failure of the venture. Difficulties may be faced in selecting employees to be placed overseas, but in a multinational organization it is not only expatriates who may experience difficulties with cultural adjustment.

The unique culture of a multinational entity will not neatly resemble a workplace in any one of the parent cultures. Rather elements of each are likely to shape different aspects of organizational activity. A clear sense of organizational goals, a strong understanding of cultural inter-play, and a carefully developed organizational strategy will make ascer-taining who is best suited to the carrying out of varied tasks easier.

The workforce in a multicultural setting is more likely to be flexible and adaptive to change if programs designed to acculturate and orient new members to the uniqueness of the practices in this venue are present. Developing these skills will be important for organizational members across the board and will enable and encourage better working relation-ships between native and expatriate workers. Careful examination of the particular needs of a specific organizational site should help point to areas in which such programs would be especially beneficial.

Evaluating Reciprocal Effects of Ventures Abroad

Just as an organization started abroad is a product of its parent cor-porations and their interaction with the national culture in which it is situated, the establishment of a site abroad typically has effects on orga-nizational culture(s) at home. As employees spend periods of time over-seas and domestic efforts are coordinated with those of sites abroad, some effects will be felt in the parent site. As always, a clear sense of pur-pose for each site will help create identification and investment by members.

If the organization's vision encompasses an international compo-nent, then the "feel" of multinationalism may pervade all organizational sites. In some ways, this may ease transitions of employees from one site to another, but in many ways it can also serve to obscure complexities. The varied national cultures in which each site is situated will undoubt-edly add nuances to behavior and influence organizational structure. Preparing employees to adjust to and understand such differences is a key role of management. It is also important to keep in mind that al-though certain structural systems may be found to be highly effective in certain sites, it will require careful assessment of cultural compatibility to ascertain their potential effectiveness in other sites.

Integrating Cultural Awareness in Daily Practice

Negotiating cultural differences is a challenge in any organizational setting. When different national cultures become implicated, the difficulties can compound themselves rapidly if a proactive approach to cultural sensitivity and awareness is not taken. Management can make a difference by clearly identifying cultural differences, articulating goals, taking culture into consideration when designing organizational structures and providing regular training and support for employees working in co-cultural environments.

Beyond this, however, a strong multinational organization integrates cultural awareness in daily practice. Leadership must continually communicate its respect for and understanding of subtle cultural differences, and this awareness must be reflected in practices and in policies. A clear sense of direction and understanding of cultural variations opens the door for management to communicate this sensitivity to the rest of the organization.

▶ Review Questions

▼ What are possible sources of culture-based difficulties in managing a multi-culturally based organization?

▼ How would you prepare an employee for a year-long period in another country?

▼ What would you consider when trying to decide how much cultural accommodation would be expected from a unit situated in another country?

▼ How would you determine how much cultural conflict is to be expected in moving operations to another country?

▼ What would you consider in developing a culture change plan for a unit in another country?

▼ What accommodations would you expect a parent company to make in initiating an overseas venture or a partnering arrangement?

▶ Discussion Questions

▼ If you work with a company with international units, how does your company address cultural differences in concepts of time, work effort, and identification with the company? If you do not work for an international organization, what are some of the problems you might expect to encounter in such a situation?

▼ What is the structure of your organization's international endeavors?

▼ How would you decide whether to use expatriate employees in your organization? If you do use expatriates, what challenges might you expect to face? How would you address them?

▼ What are the biggest challenges you would expect to face in managing a business transnationally? How are these communication problems?

▶ **Recommended Readings**

Alexander, J., & Wilson, M. (1997). Leading across cultures: Five vital capabilities. In F. Hesselbein, M. Goldsmith, & R. Beckhard (eds.), *The organization of the future.* San Francisco: Jossey-Bass.

Bartlett, C., & Ghoshal, S. (1989). *Managing across borders: The transnational solution.* Boston: Harvard Business School Press.

Fedor, K., & Werther, W., Jr. (1996, Autumn). The fourth dimension: Creating culturally responsive international audiences. *Organizational Dynamics*, pp. 39-53.

Nurmi, R., & Darling, J. (1997). International management leadership: The primary competitive advantage. New York: International Business Press.

▶ **Suggested Case Studies**

Keough, C. (1998). The case of the aggrieved expatriate. *Management Communication Quarterly, 11*(3), 453-459.

Sypher, B., Shwom, B., Boje, D., Rosile, G. A., & Miller, V. (1998). "The case of the aggrieved expatriate" analyses. *Management Communication Quarterly, 11*(3), 460-485.

Putting a Change
Process Together

Building a successful organization—and keeping it successful—requires careful attention to the workplace culture. The prior chapters have focused on the role of communication in the development, maintenance, and transformation of a company's culture. This chapter returns to some of the central themes and concepts. Partly, this is to accomplish a review and reinforcement of the development of ideas in the book as a whole. It is also intended to continue to integrate a culture-based thinking process into your ongoing practices in working in an organization. Thus, the chapter includes consideration of the functions of cultural management, the choice between leading and managing, the process of developing cases to enhance learning, and the development of continuous learning processes. Finally, these various conceptions are put into practice in consideration of a specific fully developed case.

Key Objectives of the Chapter

▼ To review basic reasons for engaging in cultural management

▼ To reconsider basic elements of cultural management

▼ To consider the choice of managing culture or leading cultural change

▼ To develop skills in writing cases involving one's own organization for the sake of examining its culture and developing interventions

▼ To look at general cultural characteristics of learning organizations

Questions to Consider

▼ Which ideas from this book have you already tried at work? How successful were your efforts? What do you believe best accounts for the degree of success or failure?

▼ Stories often clarify, reframe, and inspire. Which concepts lend themselves to "storifying"? How successful were you in constructing a story that captured the imagination of members and provided conceptual tools for change?

▼ When have you chosen to manage and support the existing culture and when have you chosen to change it? Do you think organizations engage in too many cultural change efforts? How do you know the right time to initiate change?

▼ Are you able to see the cultural logic in specific events or is it mostly a global feeling to you? When do you have time to reflect on cultural elements?

▼ Do you believe that your organization actively engages in learning and change? When does this most often occur and at what level in the organization?

▶ Looking Back

Building and maintaining an appropriate corporate culture is a key feature of building a successful business or running any organization. A positive work environment must complement a favorable market situation and skilled employees if high performance is to be achieved. Many reasons have been given for this. A positive culture increases motivation and the quality of the work effort. This shows up in a number of performance measures, including productivity and quality of relations with clients and customers.

In a turbulent business environment, continuous learning and adaptation are critical for success. Learning and adaptation require both employees' commitment to organizational objectives and employees' autonomy to take initiative and act on their own. A strong and appropriate organizational culture can resolve the potential tensions between these dual needs. Carefully integrated values enable organizational members to perceive relevant details and respond directly to events from an organizational point of view.

Cultural management enables highly effective passive control and coordination. A strong culture reduces the need for surveillance and direct supervision. This in turn reduces the cost of management and provides a more positive work environment. Decentralization, dispersed facilities, internationalization, and the need for rapid responses increases the need for cultural management, as more traditional forms of coordination and control efforts are difficult and costly to maintain.

A positive culture also increases members' identification with the organization. This increases satisfaction, reduces turnover, and improves recruitment efforts. These factors can be critical in businesses where employee qualities may be the business's greatest asset, where exiting employees carry important trade-relevant knowledge and social contacts with them, and where the competition for skilled employees is great.

▶ Managing Culture

An organization's culture impacts on employees by influencing their degree of identification with the organization, their beliefs and values, and their ways of interpreting and understanding events. Identification is accomplished through rites and rituals that increase feelings of inclusion and community and forms of explanation and justification that are well integrated with wider employee values. Beliefs and values are influenced by explicit discussion and promotion but are directed more basically by stories, values implicit in work practices, and reward systems. Interpretation and understanding are influenced by contextual frames and vocabularies as well as by beliefs and values.

These influences interact, and both the strength and content of the culture change the nature of these influences. As shown earlier, no particular cultural content is necessarily better than another. Strong cultures are not always positive. The culture has to be assessed in terms of how well the specific values and interpretive frames meet the needs of the company, employees, and external constituents. Cultural strength must be sufficient to enable identification and efficiency and yet enable alternative perspectives and consideration of alternative values, especially when product and market conditions change rapidly. As shown, cultural changes may focus on either strength or content.

Exercise 10.1

- As you think back over the various discussions in this book, what do you consider to be the most important reason to manage the culture in your own organization?

- What prior attempts to manage culture have occurred? Where did they succeed and fail? What have been the costs?

- Again assess the culture of your own organization. What do you now think of the appropriateness of its strength? Of its content?

 ## Leading and Managing

As evidenced from ancient writings forward, people have recognized that organizations need both leaders and managers. This has been expressed in the difference between prophets and priests or between inspiration and administration. Clearly, the value preference is nearly always for the former in each of these linguistic pairs. And the same has been true in this book. But equally clearly, this preference can be misguided. Many organizations have been hurt by the need some managers have to prove they are leaders. Many organizations have been reorganized and reengineered to death. Value campaigns soon fall on cynical and deaf ears.

Although the leading and managing functions are not always easily separated, different situations call for different emphases. Cultural management is an ongoing process. A positive culture is maintained through recruitment, training, and integration. No positive culture can be maintained without the mundane daily activities that support, reinforce, and reproduce that culture. Cultural management is to be emphasized when the cultural strength and content appear appropriate. The commitment of management to cultural maintenance encourages the commitment of other organizational members. Such commitment encourages efficiency and legitimacy. Cultural maintenance and development processes are as important as change processes.

Cultural leadership is called for in certain periods. Most obvious are periods of market or environmental change or major internal transitions created by mergers or leadership change. Leading a cultural change is time consuming and costly. If a new culture is to take, the campaign and commitment must be fairly complete. Faddish implementation or partial commitment usually have negative consequences. All change starts with serious assessment. Leadership is to be respected not because it is simply active but because it is active in positive and lasting ways.

▶ Writing Cases

This book has used a number of case discussions. These are important in enriching the understanding of organizational processes and in developing the application of concepts. But writing your own cases is a powerful way to assess an organization's culture and begin to develop an appropriate response to it. Writing a well-designed case helps sort out essential from less essential elements, reduces detail so focus is easier, aids the identification of underlying values, reveals interpretations, and facilitates discussion. The development of a case includes three steps.

Description of Problem and Solution

First, briefly describe a reoccurring problem the organization confronts and the way organizational members normally go about solving the problem. Include some discussion of how key members would prefer to solve the problem if they had access to the relevant people, resources, and systems.

A careful look at this description gives insight into framing processes, including the basic values and conceptions used in thinking about and assessing the organization. One can ask a number of important questions. Where did these values and conceptions come from? Who has promoted or currently promotes these values and conceptions? Would these values and conceptions be sustained if these people left? What systems reinforce the values and conceptions? What were the implied decisional premises that supported the apparently preferred choices?

What specific events have taken place in the history of the organization that have led to the "normal" way problems are approached? How functional has this way of thinking about the organization been for the organization? In what ways might the normal and idealized ways of solving the problem contribute to its continuation and generate other problems for the organization? What are the common "espoused" values and theories of how things work? What are the "values-in-use" and "theories-in-use"? To what extent do the values and conceptions identified resemble those you would find most important for the organization?

A Critical Instant

Describe in concrete detail an actual discussion or conflict situation where the identified problem was present. Include in this description an actual conversation that has taken place. Develop what was discussed earlier as a "right-hand" dialogue that reveals the likely thought process of different members. How did they interpret what was said? What is the thought process that accounts for the way they replied? What remains unsaid and potentially undiscussible? How were such things kept out of the discussion?

Were stories used? What perspectives would have to be shared for each story to make sense? What were the lessons the stories seemed to give? Were there reoccurring metaphors or slogans? If so, what were they? Why do you believe that these were present?

Which members appear to be operating with values and conceptions that differ from those you would prefer for the culture? Do they seem to recognize this gap? When personal conceptions and values differ from culturally preferred ones, there is often a gap between the "reasons" and "reasons given for" choices. Do you see any evidence for such a gap? What is it? If you were to engage in cultural change activities would others' "reasons" have to change or would changing the "reasons given" be enough? Can you change the latter without influencing the former?

Exploring Alternatives

Develop alternative problem descriptions and ways the problem could be discussed. One way to do this is to imagine the perspective of a stakeholder who is rarely included in the discussion. We have noticed, for example, that professors think far differently about university issues when their own children become students. Businesspeople often feel far differently about environmental issues when their own living community is affected. Imagining alternative perspectives helps us display values and conceptions that are hidden or so routine that they remain unnoticed.

Rewrite the dialogue using terms and concepts that both retain the basic interests of each participant and provide for a reframing of the problem. For example, Saturn had a conflict between management and labor regarding the purchasing of parts. The problem arose from the difficulties in getting high-quality parts at a target price from U.S. parts manufacturers. In a rather routine way, management wanted to purchase the parts from overseas suppliers where quality and price needs could be met. This was a market issue for them. Labor wished to buy American. This was a nationalism and group solidarity issue for them. One can easily image the rather common dispute and discussion that resulted. The problem was reframed when the discussion was changed to focusing on how to get better quality and price from U.S. manufacturers. The decision to teach parts manufacturers Saturn work processes not only achieved Saturn's objectives but had many other positive payoffs.

Unfortunately, people often have to express their interests in the available discourses (language, metaphor, concepts) in the organization. When they do so, their real interests and values are presented in distorted form and often remain obscure even to themselves. The positions they take imply proposed problem solutions but may hide more important deeper interests and make creativity in discussion difficult. Inventing new ways of talking provides the possibility for greater clarity, better understanding of perspectives, and innovation. The culture evolves in a powerful organic manner.

Two Examples

Two very brief examples illustrate how specific cases can open up the thinking about larger organizational practices from a cultural standpoint. The first comes from the university department that is the work organization of one of us and the other from a quick intervention at a convenience store.

Department Funding Discussion. From the faculty's point of view, most university departments are seriously underfunded. In our department of 16 full-time faculty, 600 undergraduate majors, and 25 doctoral students, the entire nonpersonnel budget is $30,000 a year. This is to cover all supplies, copying, postage, telephones, travel, equipment, and routine research and instructional costs.

Each year departments may request additional funding. In a good year the increase received might be 3% to 5%. Despite the small stakes, usually the funding request process is lengthy and although filled with pent-up emotion, unusually focused and rational sounding. All the various value differences in terms of commitment to different research projects, undergraduate teaching, graduate student support, and use of the copying machine are pulled out in the writing of the justification for increased funding. And much time is spent in trying to guess the university-wide priorities and the relative standing of one's own program. Most of the discussion scripts are well known, well rehearsed, time consuming, and sometimes destructive of work relations. To the members, the problem is clearly the lack of funding and the difficulty in writing the persuasive proposal that will solve the problem.

It seems clear to us, however, that the real problem is the discussion and the sustaining belief that the right discussion and proposal will finally solve the funding problem. Metaphorically, it seems to us (à la Jonathan Livingston Seagull) that this is a very time and energy consuming squabble over the scraps that keeps the group from being visionary and proactive.

One could ask the members what they would talk about if they knew that there would never be a substantial increase in funding. Perhaps predictably, several would suggest that they would have to be even clearer about their priorities so that essential activities would not be hurt. Ironically, although currently being hurt in the system, powerful people in the department may actually perceive gain by sustaining this fight. Power balances are not challenged; outcomes stay predictable. The discussion also keeps departments dependent on university sources of funding, creating control but diminishing the potential total funding for the university system. The manner of solution becomes the real problem.

A few could start to perceive a very different discussion where alternative sources of funding could be considered. The same amount of time spent on looking at new types of grant funding, partnerships with area businesses, and soliciting donations has the potential for much greater payoff. In fact, the potential for solving much of the problem as well as forging new and valuable alliances both in and outside the department resides in having this different discussion. Such a discussion could create a situation where different values and priorities reside more comfortably together.

Furthermore, one suspects that one outcome of participating in these alternative discussions and activities would ultimately result in more department funding from the university. Sometimes one best participates in the discussion by not participating in the discussion. Perhaps even more important, working out the alternatives in this case has implications for nearly all department discussions.

Making Change in a Convenience Store. A second very brief case came from a Korean American student of one of us. His father owned a convenience store in a part of a nearby city known for "racial" tensions. The store was plagued by high employee turnover and suffered from shoplifting and other problems typical of such stores. But in talking with the father it transpired that what bugged him most was that the employees (usually other ethnic minorities) working the cash register were unable to make proper change. Without totally knowing it, he used this as a kind of metaphor for slovenly behavior, low intelligence, and the sorry state of the American educational system. Everything else seemed to follow from this.

After some discussion, it was suggested that he change positions with an especially loyal but vexing employee. He would run the cash register and this employee would work on policy decisions, work schedules, product layout, and so forth. Unsurprising, he made proper change easily and even learned a thing or two about watching for shoplifting. But perhaps less expected, the employee invented a work schedule that made others happier, suggested a different placement of products that aided sales and reduced shoplifting, and even generated a list of items that would probably sell well. The problem was not the simple lack of expertise, but the failure to recognize and utilize well the expertise already present. And guess what—when the employee went back to working the cash register, making proper change was not a problem. We guess the American educational system improved.

Exercise 10.2

Write a case using an organization with which you are familiar.

- In your own case description, how does the specific way of describing and discussing the problem contribute to its continuation?

- What changes in the culture of the organizations would change the way the problem is understood? How would changing the way the problem is discussed impact on the culture?

- How would you deal with those who seem to have a way of benefiting from the continuation of the problem? What have they themselves lost in its continuation?

- Discuss the consequences of alternative way of thinking and talking.

▶ Toward a Learning Organization

Generally, the need for a specific array of cultural characteristics is dependent on industry characteristics, external values, environmental factors, and specific market conditions. Nonetheless, the capacity to learn is one cultural characteristic that may be valuable in nearly every organization. All successful organizations must continually adapt to changing conditions. As should be clear from the other chapters, independent of whatever other characteristics are present, a culture that favors adaptation is more competitive.

For years Chris Argyris has helped organizations achieve what he calls "double-loop" learning by developing a specific cultural theory-in-use. Single-loop learning is typical in organizations. It entails achieving higher competence levels in the skills and responses that already exist in the organization. Most training aims at this. Double-loop learning entails the development of different types of skills and responses.

The cultural theory-in-use of single-loop learning is fairly typical. Argyris (1992) argues that the model is governed by four variables: "(1) achieve the purpose as the actor defines it, (2) win, do not lose, (3) suppress negative feelings, and (4) emphasize rationality" (p. 218). All of these elements are clearly present in the faculty discussion described above. Although people may be very skilled in this type of discussion, rarely does it lead to organizational learning. Behaviorally, individuals engage in strategies of control and self-protection and discourage genuine inquiry.

The cultural theory-in-use of double-loop learning is quite different. The governing variables are "(1) participation of everyone in defining purposes, (2) everyone wins, no one loses, (3) express feelings, and (4) suppress the cognitive intellective aspects of action" (Argyris, 1992, p. 219). Behaviors here generally encourage inquiry, minimize unilateral control, and aim at breaking standard routines.

Many of the conceptions developed in the book as a whole have attempted to move toward a conception of organizational learning consistent with Argyris's double-loop learning. The best learning from this book is not what culture your organization should have, but how one can become a quicker and more efficient learner.

Exercise 10.3

* How would you characterize the learning style of your organization? Do individuals seek new ideas and perspectives? Does your organization try new things spontaneously or wait until moments of crisis? Is everyone a learner or only some people or groups? How does the organization store and distribute what its members have learned?

* Does your organization focus on helping people learn how to learn or on teaching specific skills? Can you think of specific instances of double-loop learning?

- Do you consider your organization to be a learning organization? What makes it so or keeps it from being so? When has learning occurred most rapidly? Most slowly?

- Does your organization have a culture of learning? What are the learning enhancing elements of its culture and the learning inhibitors?

▷ **Putting What You Know Into Practice**

The following case report is essentially the diary of a consultant hired to assist with a major cultural transformation in a public agency (our thanks to Patricia Sikora for providing the case). Please read the case and form your impressions, using where possible conceptions developed in this book. Following the case presentation will be a series of discussion questions aimed at helping you engage the case more fully.

The Case

"If you're looking at it as a solution to some communication problems between supervisors and employees, Pay for Performance doesn't change that. Unless you have a communications structure where you're committed to giving people feedback, both positive and negative, on a regular basis and supervisors with the skills to do that, you're kidding yourself if you think this is a solution to this problem. Where I used to work, I swear they went through every type of human resource planning and evaluation plan ever invented, and it all came back to: are you going to communicate with your employees. . . . unless you're committed to changing that, you're fooling yourself that any plan is going to fundamentally change how things are."

—*(Focus Group participant)*

Setting the Stage for Change

Early in 1996 a western state legislature enacted a bill mandating that all state employees be transitioned from an entitlement-based pay system to a merit-based or "pay-for-performance" system by fiscal year 2000. This new compensation approach, dubbed

"Western State Peak Performance" (WSPP), will eliminate the nearly universal and predictable annual employee raises ("step increases"), and will more closely link annual pay increases with yearly performance. The current performance evaluation system has no link to compensation, or, in some cases, actual job requirements, and will be simultaneously transformed to a more rigorous performance management system to support the documentation and managerial requirements of WSPP.

By mid-1996, a state-level Design Team was formed to make recommendations to the State Personnel Board regarding implementation of WSPP. The recommendations of the team were presented to the legislature by the State Personnel Director in October 1996. The program was strongly positioned as a major culture shift with the intent to "shift [the Western] State government to a work culture that rewards excellence in performance in order to foster a service-oriented work force as [the state] moves into the next century." Furthermore, "performance-based pay can be a powerful tool in finding new ways to make state government more citizen-oriented, responsive, flexible, and productive." The overt message throughout the report is to transform state government to a "service organization" where "citizen satisfaction is the bottom-line."

Generally the state-level plan overviews what must happen in terms of communication, training, systems, and human resource management, but provides little detail in regards to how elements of the program are to be implemented. The decision was made early by the state team that implementation of WSPP would be managed at a departmental level. That is, state-level teams and task forces (12 task forces created in late 1996) would provide general parameters and recommendations for implementation; however, specific decisions such as how to allocate funds, how/when to conduct evaluation or coaching sessions, how/what/when to communicate, what to measure, and how/when to train were to be left to individual departments.

Late in 1997, the Department of Concern Here (DOCH) initiated implementation of WSPP for the department. This department consists of approximately 550 employees in 11 autonomous divisions. It was decided that the department would utilize a cross-functional steering committee (Design Team) and six task forces (TFs) to plan and implement WSPP. Although membership in the Design Team and TFs was open to all employees, the groups were predominantly populated by directors, managers, and supervisors. Final recommendations from these groups are due June 30, 1998; implementation is to begin early 1999.

Role of Communication

Defining their role—therefore the role of communication—was the overt "problem" for the Communication Task Force. Except for the very first meeting, virtually every meeting of the Communication Task Force was dominated by disagreement/debate over what the task force should or should not do. Although this was sometimes couched in terms of how much effort people were willing to invest to "do" communications, much of the difficulty in moving ahead was due to differences in perspectives about the role of communication in the change process. In fact, choices (lack of choices) about communication contributed significantly to the maintenance of the status quo and raised early barriers to organizational transformation.

Process or Content

One unspoken question in the meetings was: is communication a noun or a verb? a what or a how? In an early Communication Task Force meeting (2/24) a list was "brainstormed" around what aspect of communication the team might focus on: creating, relaying, editing, consulting, planning, integrating, packaging, distributing, soliciting, eliciting, defending, etc. Although all of these were expressed as verbs, there were two separate paths described by the team: (a) developing and editing content, or (b) distributing and delivering messages. The former required that the team write its own material or substantially edit minutes/documents from the other TFs. The latter implied a more passive, reactive role where the team would simply take what was developed by other groups and act as a delivery system.

Definitions of quality entered into this debate as those who advocated the "content" approach felt that quality of communication hinged on appropriate packaging, integration, or distillation of messages, whereas the "process" members felt that quality information was the "pure," accurate, and timely message "direct from the horse's mouth."

> "The Communication Task Force will create a plan to communicate DOCH Peak Performance developments to all DOCH employees in a timely, accurate, and understandable manner using various mediums." (3/3—Communication Task Force)

In the end, the "conduit" metaphor prevailed, not only because it involved less time and responsibility for individual members, but because it was most congruent with "how we do things around here." The conduit approach maintained the isolation of groups from each other, kept the focus away from the creation of new meaning, and kept power and authority relationship static. By focusing only on the process and defining their output in terms of guidelines or plans, the Communication Task Force did not have to get its hands dirty with the real work of creating meaning for the organization.

Integrated or Separate

In addition to the question of whether the function of the Communication Task Force was to generate content or process, there was implicit disagreement as to whether communication was a separate task or was to be an integral part of the entire WSPP process. Creating a separate "task" force immediately set communication as "separate from" other activities.

Initial discussions regarding the role of the Communication Task Force did, however, revolve around integrating or, at least, orchestrating various messages across the other TFs and Design Team. That is, the "ideal" communication process was defined in terms of integrating communication into every aspect of the process and ensuring that input from as well as messages to employees were tightly woven into decisions made by the Design Team and TFs.

Some Communication Task Force members, then, defined their role as consultants to the TFs and advocated a more cross-functional or "communication is organizing" approach to WSPP planning and operations:

"It can't be a communications plan without us being involved in decisions—communications influences everything: how decisions are made as well as the timing, the message, or the medium." (2/24—Communication Task Force)

Very quickly, however, this position was overwhelmed by those who wanted to draw clearer lines between roles and "tasks" associated with communication. Communication was piecemealed into discrete elements that different groups should or could own: Who should write content? Who should approve content? Who should integrate across the groups? Who should respond to employees? Who should set up the email system? Who should edit TF minutes? Even as the "central importance" of communication to the WSPP process was emphasized, it became fragmented into a haphazard list of tasks, some of which were assigned, whereas others were not.

"Communication is so centrally important, it really should be coming from the Design Team. Our role could be planning and strategies, but approval, clearinghouse, oversight role should be Design Team." (3/31—Communication Task Force)

"I think we should not address 'whole' communications issues. That is the Design Team's job." (4/14—Communication Task Force)

"Isn't it our responsibility to do Q&A? I'm having trouble w/where our role ends. That isn't our role. But where does it happen then?" (4/14—Communication Task Force)

"If we're there, we'll be assigned the role of writing communications, we'll end up doing it for the TF. We'd be setting up the expectation that we'd do their job." (2/24—Communication Task Force)

The theme of "It's not my job" emerged in the Communication Task Force by mid-March. By dissecting communication into piece-parts, responsibilities could be delegated or abdicated more easily to others. Over the course of 2 months, integrated, coherent communication to and from employees about WSPP fell by the wayside as individuals debated over "whose job" it was to handle discrete aspects of communication.

The Communication Task Force was successful in convincing the Design Team that the TFs should have the responsibility for communicating their "news" within the broad parameters of "the Communication Task Force guidelines." As a result, little or no strategic communication was developed, interactions between task forces were limited, information that was critical to share was not shared, and decisions remained narrowly constrained by the perspectives of those serving on the Design Team and TFs.

Authority to Communicate

"Which model do they want us to be? They want us to decide. How can we decide? We have to discuss and come to consensus. We need to clarify though if Design Team wants x or y." (2/24—Communication Task Force)

"Do we want influence before or after the communications is developed? I just don't think we have the authority to tell TFs what to do. We can decide to have that authority. We can make recommendations, but can't have veto power; that's the Design Team role." (2/24—Communication Task Force)

Many early Communication Task Force discussions revolved around "them": What did they want? When will they tell us what to do? When will they get their job done so we can do ours? They know what they want, why won't they tell us? They told us to write a plan, and so forth. There was confusion as well as dissension regarding what authority the TF had to act on its own recommendations.

Initial meeting minutes noted that one of the members was going to attempt to get on a division directors' (DDs) meeting agenda and discuss the level of authority the team had so it could act without "being bogged down by a bureaucratic process of clearing every idea with the Design Team and DDs" (2/11—Communication Task Force). That meeting apparently never happened, and discussions around power and authority continued until the group was forced into action by "them," that is, the Design Team lost patience with the "dysfunctional" Communication Task Force and mandated a set of guidelines for communication.

The Communication Task Force, although overtly charged with the responsibility to develop and implement a communication plan, could not resolve internal conflict over how much authority it really had. It was obvious that several members still operated under traditional hierarchical power assumptions: They were very uncomfortable issuing any guidelines or taking on any task without first obtaining approval from an "official" person or group. Others in the group believed, or wanted to believe, that the Communication Task Force was charged both with the responsibility and the authority to direct and manage communication for the WSPP process.

Lack of agreement around this issue severely hampered creative thinking and action in the Communication Task Force. If an idea or approach did not fit in an existing box or set of well-defined parameters, it was quickly snuffed out or tabled until approval could be sought. Often, approval required weeks of waiting, and by the time the rubber stamp was obtained, the opportunity was lost or timing of communication out of sync with the process. Those who had joined the group ready to "dive in and do something" were extremely frustrated and often "shut down" as their ideas were continually dismissed as not within the realm of the team's authority. This was unfortunate as these were the individuals that tended to have the most to contribute in terms of experience and innovation.

"When I volunteered I thought we'd be making a real communications plan, now I've done a 180. I don't want an approval role, I don't want my name associated with communications if I'm not responsible for it. We're just the delivery system. Get a mailman, then, if you're just talking delivery system, not a communications plan. I don't want to be a mailman, I want a true plan." (3/10—Communication Task Force)

What Is WSPP? Sense Making in Teams

What message? A critical meeting was the Design Team meeting held on March 9. At this meeting, each TF reported on its progress. Virtually every TF reported that it was struggling with roles, purpose, and objectives, and had yet to get out of a "hashing out the same old stuff" mode. When the Communication Task Force reported that it was having similar problems, Design Team members were visibly more distressed than when the other TFs had made their reports. This might have been partially due to the more detailed account given by the Communication Task Force spokesperson of personnel problems (members dropping out, difficulty getting the same people in the same meetings) and conflicts occurring in the meetings.

The overt concern was that "such a critical team would be so dysfunctional." At this point, communication to employees was still viewed as a primary task and there was great concern that the Communication Task Force had not yet sent out a message about WSPP or, at least, created a plan to do so. What virtually no one acknowledged, however, was there was no message to send. Through out the entire chain of players involved with WSPP, from top state groups through the departmental task forces, there had yet to be any interactive sense making around WSPP.

Leadership and Sense Making

"The Design Team isn't doing their job. The Design Team wants us to create a message, but they haven't given us the message. The Design Team doesn't know what it wants. The Design Team wants us to be their communicator. Isn't overall communications the job of the Design Team? We just need to make some decisions about the 'whats.'" (3/10—Communication Task Force)

"I wish someone would just say, 'we don't know.' You're not going to see that, everyone is walking around saying, 'we don't know,' but no one is willing to come out and say it. Yeah, so this uncomfortable sense persists." (3/31—Communication Task Force)

The Communication Task Force was given the responsibility to create a message in a sense-making vacuum. The only "sense" or meaning that had been officially crafted was generally viewed with cynicism and distrust (the "vision" articulated by the state-level team—see "Setting the Stage for Change") No one believed this vision. It was typically viewed as a facade for the "real" vision: cutting costs and eliminating jobs.

The individuals on this TF had neither the skills nor the experience in crafting a compelling strategic level vision for the department. In fact, it is rarely the role of a team or task force to create such a message or "make sense" for an organization. Typically, ad hoc teams are brought together for very specific, tactical problem solving or implementation of solutions. Labeling the "problem" or articulating the vision is the traditional role of senior management sources.

Organizational life revolves as much around the framing or definition of problems (even though this may be implicit or "by default") as it does around decisions. Before a problem can be solved, the leader first draws attention to specific things, create boundaries around what is or is not believed to be relevant, imposes some sort of coherence on it, and finally names it: competitive threat, customer satisfaction, productivity improvement, and so on. Staff or teams are then able to move forward with at least a minimal level of shared understanding of what "it" is.

The only high-level "naming" that has occurred around WSPP had been done by groups whose credibility was highly suspect: the Legislature and highest levels of Personnel. Sense giving around a fundamental culture shift had been delegated not to just one team, but dozens of teams (if one includes the state-level "guideline" teams and task forces). The Design Team and Communication Task Force were implicitly charged with a leadership role in providing "sense" to the organization, but were hampered in doing so not only due to lack of skill and experience, but, as noted in the next section, lack of opportunity.

Meetings and Sense Making

> "The Design Team has really shifted into information gathering rather than being a steering committee. . . . It's hard to do things in a committee of 16 that meets every two weeks. It would be easier if we had 2 or 3 people who would take the bull by the horns." (4/14—Communication Task Force)

Meetings are where sense happens. This is where the creative potential of "intersubjective" or interactional sense making comes up against the controlling orientation of generic subjectivity. Generic meanings are those implicit organizational assumptions, scripts, and norms about "how we do things" that maintain the stability of the organization (the term generic is used because, in fact, meanings are removed from the individual or "subject" and have become objectified or reified as operating "truth").

In times of stability, generic subjectivity is very functional; when times change, however, old scripts may no longer be viable and new meanings need to emerge from interactions or intersubjective sense making. In effect, new shared meanings cannot emerge unless new meanings are shared among individuals.

This transition from old to new requires face-to-face, "messy" interactions around assumptions, beliefs, and norms. But in most organizations, there is a strong bias against meetings: meetings are to be as infrequent, as short, and as structured (i.e., efficient) as possible. There was a strong bias against meetings evident from the beginning of the WSPP process. Several groups—the Design Team and four of six TFs—tried to move as quickly as possible to an every other week or ad hoc meeting schedule.

The Communication Task Force was one of the few groups that immediately went to a 1.5-hour meeting instead of a 2-hour meeting schedule. Attendance at meetings was spotty at best. Very few individuals attended every meeting (only one person in the Communication Task Force had attended every meeting through mid-May); arriving late and leaving early were common patterns. Very frequently, at the end of meetings a request would be made such as "Do you think we can start meeting just once a month now?" or "When this plan is done we don't have to meet any more, right?" The vehicle for intersubjective sense making was shunned or stigmatized as a necessary evil.

Conflict suppression and non-sense making: Meetings that did occur were tightly controlled by agendas and dominated by unidirectional information sharing and formal presentations. Opportunities to express opinions, get conflicting assumptions on the table, or obtain diverse perspectives were rarely "on the agenda." Conflict, in fact, did not seem to have a place in most of the meetings. It was rare for individuals to openly disagree with each other.

Sometimes one or two people would make a comment or ask a polite question of a speaker, but there seemed to be unspoken norms of "niceness" that would not allow "tough" questions or "out-of-bounds" comments within the confines of the meetings. Most of the debate between team members occurred via email exchanges or in small, ad hoc groups of two or three members. These debates were rarely brought into regular meetings for group discussion.

The few times when tempers "flared" in the Design Team were when nonmembers attended the meetings. These were often individuals who were not managers or not part of the "inner circle" of departmental leaders. These individuals, not being familiar with taboo subjects or unwritten rules, would typically be the ones to question underlying assumptions or ask, "Why does it have to be like this?" Often, after some polite response, the topic was changed and the question buried or tabled until next meeting, where it would be tabled yet again.

Resistance to "real" input seemed high, and Design Team members seemed to prefer the "path of least resistance." This was in part due to the executive director's emphasis on speed and minimal investment of resources. Members were quite skilled at conflict suppression, however; the ease at which conflict was avoided implied that this was common practice rather than unique behavior.

The Communication Task Force may have been viewed as "dysfunctional" because in initial meetings, there were no agendas, discussion got very heated around the role of communications, and people were very honest (and uncomfortable) about the "messiness" of the meetings. Instead of being dysfunctional, the team, in fact, was wrestling with fundamental assumptions and norms and was proceeding down the path of intersubjective sense making.

The timeline and organizational norms would not allow the "messiness" to continue, however. People who could not handle the level of conflict in the Communication Task Force quickly dropped out of the group. The remaining members, after a particularly intense interaction, decided to create "operating principles" to better manage the meetings. At this point, agendas were mandated, roles assigned, and members admonished to "be respectful"; meetings were essentially sanitized to reduce friction. Simultaneously, in the Design Team the task force was labeled "dysfunctional" and told to "get back to business" and write a plan.

Sense making in the Communication Task Force abated at this point only to rear its head again after the plan was written and it became evident that a plan was not communication. The April 14 minutes note:

"Some members believed a more intensive hands-on approach was necessary to ensure all DOCH employees were aware of WSPP developments and communications. Further discussion will continue on this subject at the next Communication Task Force meeting after the current communications plan has been in use for one month." (4/14—Communication Task Force)

Despite an attempt to table this discussion yet again, a handful of individuals—those who originally viewed communication as (a) meaning/content-based, (b) a "whole" effort rather than piecemeal tasks, and (c) integral to the entire change process—continued to push for "real" communication. This group plans to form a new Communication Task Force "subgroup" to initiate what has been termed "Phase 2" of the Communication Task Force mission: develop two-way communication channels, integrate messages across the TFs, and provide consultive support to the TFs and Design Team. The symbol metaphor may yet have an opportunity to emerge.

SOURCE: This case was developed by Patricia B. Sikora. Used with permission.

Discussion Questions

▼ Describe the culture at this state agency the best you can from the brief description here. How would you classify it based on the typologies given in Chapter 1?

▼ Describe in contrast the envisioned culture. How would it differ in authority relations, site of responsibility, and feelings toward tasks?

▼ Describe the assumptions about people and work built into both cultures. Do you perceive any gaps between the espoused values and assumptions and the implicit ones driving decisions in either the present or the envisioned culture?

▼ Reconstruct the view of the change process from the point of view of the state, the upper managers, and then most of the members on the task forces. In what ways are these similar and different?

▼ What are the leading sources of resistance to this change process?

▼ How well designed do you consider the change process to be? Where is it strong? Where is it weak?

▼ How would you cast the vision that appears to be present? Do you think that it was clear and compelling to members? Could it have been made so?

▼ Based on the information here, how congruent would you say the cultural change is with the other practices in the organization?

▼ Do you think that the Design Team (the leading coalition for change) was well chosen? What would you have considered in addition to what the management there did?

▼ Much was made in the case about sense making. Chapter 4 developed this as a problem of aligning interpretive frames. Where were events and expectations given different interpretations?

▼ Framing seemed to be a constant problem in this organization. What framing options would you consider to better manage meaning through this change?

▼ What do you make of the conflict on the metaphor for communication? Was this a trivial issue? What difference would the metaphor make?

▼ At least on the surface, upper management seemed committed to empowerment and widespread participation, yet this did not seem to generate either commitment or good ideas. Based on the information given here why do you think that happened?

▼ The meetings often seemed to be a waste. Do you see evidence of "discussions" or "dialogues"? What would have been different if the mix of these two was different?

▼ Make a recommendation to the management of this agency. How should the change effort be handled from this point forward?

▼ This is a major transition for a state agency. Do you think that cultural issues were adequately considered? Where they were considered were genuine differences recognized and appreciated?

▼ Questions of ethics never arose in the various discussions recorded here. Do you think there were important ethical questions that went unaddressed? Which and where?

▶ Review Questions

▼ Why has cultural management become of such concern to successful organizations today?

▼ Ideally, what functions are achieved by successful cultural management?

▼ Why was managing culture considered to be as important as leading cultural change? Or why is riding waves often more successful than making them?

▼ What are the elements of a well-written case?

▼ What can one learn by writing cases about one's own organization?

▼ What is meant by double-loop learning? What is the cultural theory-in-use that supports it?

▶ Reference and Recommended Reading

Argyris, C. (1992). *On organizational learning*. Cambridge, MA: Blackwell Business.

Index

▼

About the Authors

▼

Stanley A. Deetz, Ph.D., is Professor of Communication at the University of Colorado, Boulder, where he teaches courses in organizational theory, organizational communication, and communication theory. He is the author of *Transforming Communication, Transforming Business: Building Responsive and Responsible Workplaces* (1995) and *Democracy in an Age of Corporate Colonization: Developments in Communication and the Politics of Everyday Life* (1992), coauthor of *Doing Critical Management Research* (in press), and editor or author of 10 other books. He has published numerous essays in scholarly journals and books regarding stakeholder representation, decision making, culture, and communication in corporate organizations and has lectured widely in the United States and Europe. In 1994, he was a Senior Fulbright Scholar in the Företagsekonomiska Institutionen, Göteborgs Universitet, Sweden, lecturing and conducting research on managing knowledge-intensive work. He has served as a consultant on culture, diversity, and participatory decision making for several major corporations. He served as President of the International Communication Association, 1996-1997.

Sarah J. Tracy is a doctoral candidate in the Department of Communication at the University of Colorado, Boulder. She has published essays in *Human Communication Research* and the *Journal of Applied Communica-*

tion regarding discourse and emotional management in organizations. She also works as a consultant using performance and humor as change and training approaches.

Jennifer Lyn Simpson is a doctoral student in the Department of Communication at the University of Colorado, Boulder. She is currently engaged in a major research project for the university studying its diversity programs focusing on the consequences of different discursive forms on decision making.